*The Battleground
of the Curriculum*

W. B. CARNOCHAN

The Battleground of the Curriculum

Liberal Education and
American Experience

Stanford University Press
Stanford, California
1993

Stanford University Press
Stanford, California
© 1993 by the Board of Trustees of the
Leland Stanford Junior University
Printed in the United States of America

CIP data appear at the end of the book

For Kate and Patrick
(and their generation)

Preface

If it had not been for six years I spent at the Stanford Humanities Center as its director, I would not have attempted this book. Only the challenge and stimulus of many a conversation with many an acquaintance, old and new, gave me the sense that it might be done—even though my professional life has been largely spent in the environs of the eighteenth century. To the fellows of the Center in those six years, I owe a great deal. But not more than I also owe the Center's staff. Not only was (and is) it the best I have known, it is the best I could imagine. Working with Sue Dambrau and Susan Sebbard, whom I single out because both were at the Center during all my years there, was a rare pleasure. Their skill, energy, patience, and tolerance for foible have been of untold help to many students, to many scholars, and to me. Others to whom I am grateful are Dee Marquez, Margaret Seligson, and Ellen Schwerin. The Center was crucial to the enterprise of this book; to be there was to see new avenues of possibility.

Another debt of long standing is to the staff of the Stanford University Libraries. Too many people have been too helpful for too long for me to name them all here. But Margaret Kimball deserves special thanks for sleuthing that located archival material relating to the history of Stanford's curriculum. Elisabeth Green was particularly helpful in the search for the elusive father of "Civics," Henry Randall Waite. I also take the chance to thank Michael Ryan, whose learning and inventiveness have added much to the university's intellectual life. Stanford is losing Michael Ryan to the University of Pennsylvania. It is Pennsylvania's gain, Stanford's loss. My thanks also to archivists at Harvard and to Rhea Pliakis, of Columbia, for responding so efficiently to requests for help and information.

While working on this book, I may sometimes have resembled the ancient mariner, stopping one in three. All I can say in defense is that I have benefited greatly from the knowledge and insight of others, among whom I can name Carl Degler, Kenneth Fields, Lilian Furst, Elisabeth Hansot, N. Katherine Hayles, Alan Heimert, Barry Katz, David Kennedy, Sheldon Rothblatt, and Bernard Siegel—with apologies to any who should be on the list but aren't, thanks to the incapacities of memory. The associate directors of the Humanities Center during my time there, Charles Junkerman and Morton Sosna, discovered that one of their responsibilities not in the job description was to listen to me trying out ideas; they always had knowledge of their own to add to my store. To David Tyack, George Dekker, and James Sheehan, I am grateful for readings of the manuscript that have improved it immeasurably. Jeffrey Erickson's work as a research assistant was thorough and helpful.

For the Stanford University Press, I have nothing but praise, especially for Helen Tartar. There could be no more creative, thoughtful, and generous an editor. I thank her both for help with this book and for what she has contributed to the growth of the Press. At a point in Stanford's recent budget crises, the Press came under threat. Catastrophe was averted in part because of Helen Tartar's success in building the Press's strength and standing in the area of the humanities. Nancy Atkinson was a thoughtful and meticulous copy editor, whose work was in keeping with the Press's high standards. John Feneron saw the book through production with his customary good humor and finesse.

I also should acknowledge two intellectual debts. The first is to the late Michel Foucault. But those who do not count themselves disciples of Foucault need not, I think, take alarm. The recognition that the power of (for example) academic departments exercises itself in subtle ways, though owing something in my case to Foucault's insights, demands no systematic acceptance of Foucault's thought. The second debt is to Hugh Hawkins's study, *Between Harvard and America: The Educational Leadership of Charles W. Eliot*, on which I have often relied in trying to understand the intellectual milieu of Harvard's most influential president.

Finally, there are debts of life larger than (though often inseparable from) those of work. Thanks to my children, Lisa, Sarah, Peter, and Sibyll, and to Erika Fields, for goodness of spirit (and for keeping me younger than otherwise I might be); to my grandchildren, Kate and Patrick, for a glimpse of the future; and to Brigitte, for more than I can name.

W.B.C.

Contents

I.   Prologue   1

II.   Charles Eliot and James McCosh:
The Free Elective System vs. a "Trinity"
of Studies   9

III.   Ancients, Moderns, and the Rise of
Liberal Education   22

IV.   Two Strains of Humanism: *The Idea of
a University* and *Culture and Anarchy*   39

V.   "Great Changes Are Impending":
The Politics of Counter-revolution,
1884–1909   51

VI.   Between the Wars: Aspirations to Order   68

VII.   General Education "in a Free Society":
Harvard's Redbook, the "1960s," and
the Image of Democracy   88

VIII. Orbs, Epicycles, and the Wars
of "Culture"   100

IX.   What to Do?   112

       Appendix. Edgar Eugene Robinson,
       "Citizenship in a Democratic World"
       (1928)   129

       Notes   147

       Works Cited   155

       Index   167

In a general way, the place of the university in the culture of Christendom is still substantially the same as it has been from the beginning. Ideally, and in the popular apprehension, it is, as it has always been, a corporation for the cultivation and care of the community's highest aspirations and ideals. But these ideals and aspirations have changed somewhat with the changing scheme of the Western civilization; and so the university has also concomitantly so changed in character, aims and ideals as to leave it still the corporate organ of the community's dominant intellectual interest. At the same time, it is true, these changes in the purpose and spirit of the university have always been, and are always being, made only tardily, reluctantly, concessively, against the protests of those who are zealous for the commonplaces of the day before yesterday. Such is the character of institutional growth and change; and in its adaptation to the altered requirements of an altered scheme of culture the university has in this matter been subject to the conditions of institutional growth at large. An institution is, after all, a prevalent habit of thought, and as such is subject to the conditions and limitations that surround any change in the habitual frame of mind prevalent in the community.

Thorstein Veblen,
The Higher Learning in America (1918)

I

Prologue

Once upon a time, so legend goes, all was harmony in the American curriculum, a time of accepted values, practices, texts; it was a golden age. This legend is simply wrong. More accurately—and to shift the metaphorical ground—the present condition of the curriculum in American higher education resembles that of a fault system still heaving and buckling with aftershocks of an earlier, larger rupture. That earlier rupture came in the context of a new creation, for the late nineteenth century saw the birth of the American university: a blend of European example and American practice, touched by the almost invisible hand of social Darwinism yet also by the habit of American egalitarianism, a volatile combination of meritocracy and democracy, an adaptive response to the heterogeneity of an immigrant society, and (nonetheless) an institution seeking to preserve the values—associated since the late eighteenth and early nineteenth centuries with the universities of Oxford and Cambridge—of "liberal education." Out of such a mixture, conflict was inescapable. And out of it there came many years later, as one example among others, the struggle over "Western Culture" at Stanford University that caught the attention of the politically ambitious and of the nation as well.

Education exercises a fascination on the American mind that stood out once more when George Bush said he wanted to be the "education president." Yet as a product of our particular history and culture, the practices of education, or at least of higher education, go insufficiently examined. How did we find ourselves where we are? What historical forces have been at work behind debates that have had an oddly airless character, as though what was being debated had never been debated before? And what might be gained by sharper answers to these questions? Much, I think.

To realize (for example) that certain conceptual origins of liberal education in its modern sense, that central building block of American higher education, lie within our historical reach, that it is not the unconditional or transhistorical value it is sometimes said to be, and that it has gathered to itself so many accretions of idea and value—so many distinguishable functions that have nonetheless become extremely difficult to distinguish—none of this need undermine its value. Such realizations can make it easier to think about liberal education more practically and more constructively, easier to find out what liberal education in the American context actually means and how it actually works, easier to separate out separate strands, and easier to analyze ways in which it might work better.

In matters of the American curriculum, the long, powerful tenure of Charles William Eliot as president of Harvard offers a starting point, even though Eliot has sometimes received more credit for introducing the free elective system than was his due (much to the exasperation, for example, of Cornell's first president, Andrew Dickson White). But his program was so far-reaching and his tenure so long that American higher education has never been the same after him, just as events in France in 1789—no matter what reversals followed eventually—unalterably changed the political and social landscape. At the same time, beginning with Eliot means beginning, in one sense, in the middle of things. Though his allegiance was more to the German than to the English system of university education, the values (and the romance) of Oxford and Cambridge were inescapably part of American longings for a usable past; beginning with Eliot will therefore require a subsequent look backward to Britain at the turn of the nineteenth century and then to John Henry Newman and to Matthew Arnold, in whom Eliot's opponents, whose strength gathered as his 40-year tenure came to its end, placed much of their trust.

Occupying Harvard's presidency from 1869, when he was 35, to 1909, when he was 75, Eliot fought a relentless, controversial, and successful battle to break down the prescribed curriculum and install the free elective system, in which students were able to set their own programs almost at will. Recognizing a national impulse to loosen the reins of dogmatic authority and admit a more entrepreneurial spirit, he translated this spirit of the times radically into educational action. Indeed he could be thought responsible, even at this distance of time, for the present "crisis" of the curriculum, insofar as "multiculturalism," with its plural values, depends on a curriculum in which subjects can be added incrementally to an existing body of knowledge. Yet Eliot remained loyal to the idea of liberal education even while taking measures that aimed, his enemies were to say, at its destruction. He believed he was proposing nothing more than "the enlargement of the circle of liberal arts" and the strengthening of the foundations of democratic society.[1]

The "crisis" of the curriculum and liberal education has been going on for a long time, and crisis-mongering has become a national pastime. In Allan Bloom's *The Closing of the American Mind* (1987), the "crisis" of the university serves as a springboard to the larger crisis of everything: "the crisis of liberal education is a reflection of a crisis at the peaks of learning, an incoherence and incompatibility among the first principles with which we interpret the world, an intellectual crisis of the greatest magnitude, which constitutes the crisis of our civilization." Crisis sells books, and seldom has a "crisis" so badly needed the protective embrace of quotation marks as that of the present curricular disputes. Commentators, typically but not exclusively American, have sometimes remarked this crisis-mongering agenda. John Searle said in 1990, "I cannot recall a time when American education was not in a 'crisis.'" Another observer (not American) wrote in 1983, "In recent years much ink has been shed to the effect that a 'crisis' is besetting the study of English literature, . . . [but] this is nothing new." And while serving in the 1960s as a "committee of one" to study general education at Columbia, Daniel Bell wrote, "General education, we are told, is in a state of 'crisis'"; he added, "in the American temper, a problem is often seen as a crisis." So pervasive is the crisis mentality when it comes to education that debunking it can also become habitual. Still, it needs to be done. Crises engender panic and call for heroic responses. Problems call for solutions—or for accommodations.[2]

The history of the American college and university from the beginning has been told by Frederick Rudolph, as has the history of the curriculum; the emergence of the research university in the late nineteenth century has been described in patient detail by Laurence Veysey; and two volumes of documentation from the seventeenth century on have been collected by Richard Hofstadter and Wilson Smith. Yet a fuller sense of the history of the university and its curriculum as an ongoing intellectual episode, subject to the same sort of scrutiny and analysis as any other long-term struggle of contested ideas, is badly needed. It is unsurprising that political actors in these struggles are—or at least give no evidence that they are not—ignorant of the university's past; a knowledge of the actual past might compromise its representation. It is more surprising that university faculties also lack a firm historical sense of how the character of American universities is bound up with major currents of nineteenth-century thought, with the egalitarian heterogeneity and social imperatives of American life, or with educational change in nineteenth-century Britain; and even of how curricular wars that have come and gone have arisen from discordances in the body politic—an issue that, though patently on the surface in one sense, is only faintly understood in its historical aspect.

If any version of the universities' history is widely known and shared, it is that in the late nineteenth century the German model was imported and "research" came to center stage. That is not untrue, only insufficient. Having spent time in Marburg and regarding the German system as only a partial model for what he wanted to achieve, namely, a combination of university and college, Eliot the Boston-bred Unitarian had a homegrown sense of social responsibility and American tradition. Indeed the radical thoroughness of his reforms, presented as a matter of plainest common sense, was deeply in the American grain, arising from a combination of forward-lookingness and a desire to preserve. When he urged enlarging "the circle of the liberal arts," Eliot was not just paying lip service to the ideal that his own reforms seemed to place in jeopardy. "Liberal education," he said, "is not safe and strong in a country in which the great majority of the men who belong to the intellectual professions are not liberally educated." And that, he said, "is just the case in this country." By free election, he hoped not so much to create a "research university" as to make liberal education safe and strong.[3]

However numerous the trials of American higher education, and however unstable it may seem in the aftershocks of the nineteenth-century rupture, these trials and instabilities—in addition to the incomparable prosperity, now perhaps at an end, of the society—have given it in this century tensility and strength. Some of the vitality of the American university has been fostered by the often unseemly squabbling and conspicuous wringing of hands that have been among its distinguishing marks. But we have reached a situation of diminishing returns in which the apparent sameness of the argument undermines some of its vitality (if not its volume), even its interest, while obscuring the possibility of an analysis that would distinguish what is merely repetitious from what is—however analogous to earlier debate—qualitatively different and dependent on new circumstances in the society. Without clearer analysis, American higher education risks the danger of seeming to repeat itself, perhaps to the point of exhaustion.

Are there any ways out of this thicket? I believe there are. One is that of further historical work, both in the style of panorama and at the level of conceptual inquiry. The belief that "liberal education" is a transhistorical value has impeded the habit of doing what universities usually do best, namely, studying currents and crosscurrents of change over time. With better conceptual understanding, a second avenue to change presents itself: a clearer sense, potentially, of purpose. What exactly is liberal education *for?* It is lamented often enough, but seldom more than lamented, that we really seem not to know, at least not very well, what we are trying to do. Third, with better conceptual understanding, we can better respond to local circumstance rather than assuming—when it comes to liberal education—that there is only a single desirable formula and that what is good for one is equally good for all. If it serves its purpose, this book should make others want to go farther. Should a disclaimer be needed, I make no pretense of being a historian, and what follows, except in the final section, is a series of time exposures, excerpting events and ideas over the last 200 years. In the final section, I consider in more but not extensive detail directions that I think would be helpful.

If a *real* crisis now exists, or threatens to, it is that the squabbling and wringing of hands have become so much a routinized exercise as to obscure what is actually taking place on the intellectual landscape. Max Weber described as the "routinization" of charisma the decline of personal leadership into bureaucracy and officialdom. If the debate about the curriculum becomes just a strategic ground on which to argue out social divisions rather than a serious effort to deal with the theory and practice of education itself—if, that is, the political content of the debate becomes its only driving force—so much will have been lost that one might then want to speak of a crisis without the embrace of quotation marks.

In an essay on these matters, Louis Menand has said that the university is not set up "to discover ways of correcting inequities and attitudes that persist in the society as a whole."[4] This is a wise reminder. At the same time, it discounts the sense of civic and moral obligation that has driven American higher education since Harvard was founded, in 1636, to ensure the survival of a learned clergy and that has merged, though not without awkwardness, with the ideal of liberal education.[5] It discounts, that is, the belief system within which American higher education operates, a system that has produced a host of tensions. This book aims to recapture certain contexts from which our present discontents, with all their political colorations, have sprung and to suggest not the way out but how we might look for a way.

Finally, I should declare not my interest but the boundaries of my own experience, which determine in part the limits of this book. The two universities I know best are Harvard and Stanford, the one where I spent eleven years as a student and a junior-level administrator, the other where I have taught and done some other things since 1960. And, while Harvard and Stanford have played a considerable role in the history of American higher education, they are obviously not the whole story. In a recent reexamination of "the idea of the university," Jaroslav Pelikan, of Yale, singles out three nineteenth-century university presidents as deserving special mention: Daniel Coit Gilman, of Johns Hopkins; Andrew Dickson White, of Cornell; and William Rainey Harper, of Chicago.[6] Eliot of Harvard is not on the list, a mark of how many different stories of the American university can be told. Moreover, the tendency to tell the story as that of the American *private* university, though not without some reasons behind it, is also limiting. Someone whose experience had been at the Universities of Michigan and California would see things differently. Since I value the determinants of the local, I make no apology for those that are present here but welcome any shadings of emphasis or outright corrections that others may offer.

II

Charles Eliot and James McCosh

The Free Elective System vs. a 'Trinity' of Studies

Until Eliot's revolution, freshmen at Harvard were required to take a wholly prescribed curriculum—including Latin, Greek, mathematics, French, elocution, ethics, and Victor Duruy's *Histoire Grecque*—and to be conversant with twenty chapters of Gibbon's *Decline and Fall of the Roman Empire* as well as some 350 pages of the Scottish philosopher Dugald Stewart. Sophomores took physics, chemistry, German, elocution, and "themes." In addition both freshmen and sophomores had some electives. In the last two years, other possibilities of choice were introduced, but the principle of prescription remained.[1] By the time Eliot had finished his work, only freshman English and another language in the freshman year were required. Otherwise, students could graduate with any combination of courses, subject to the condition that they progress from less to more advanced; they could not, as is now often the case in fields lacking an obvious progression of learning, take (say) "English 200" before taking "English 10." And around the idea of the free elective system, Eliot spun a rhetoric and ideology that still mark the American university, even among those who may reject conclusions that Eliot himself derived. Like other successful reformers, Eliot adjusted his reforms to a system of social reference: what could be more desirable, in the American democracy, than what is elective, free, and supportive of initiative and self-reliance?

But like other reformers, Eliot had no easy time of it, and outside of Harvard, the free elective system never prevailed so completely or for so long. In 1885 there occurred a debate that in tone and character summed up the issues and in effect established an agenda for the next century. It pitted Eliot against a formidable opponent, President James McCosh of Princeton, each defending values that they invested with an aura of the sacred. What shines forth from the encounter is this interplay and opposition of the secular and the sacred, with its anticipation of a not always explicit, but almost always present, issue in the educational contests of this century. In the aftermath of Stanford's latest curricular debate, Herbert Lindenberger published an article that he called "On the Sacrality of Reading Lists"; the title gets at persistent undertones of feeling that accompany ostensibly secular questions of the curriculum. The belief in the sacredness of learning has in this country never been entirely lost.[2]

The encounter between Eliot and McCosh took place at a private house in Manhattan, under the auspices of the Nineteenth Century Club, and became the occasion of discussion, in the words of Princeton's historian, "from one end of the country to another"—with a consensus of opinion behind McCosh.[3] The national prominence of this debate helps explain the national prominence of the one that followed a century later: these matters engage the American mind at a level where understanding yields to instinct and instinct is then buttressed by argument, all of it serving as an ongoing national referendum, not only about national programs but about national purposes and the foundations of American social experience.

Laying out the basis of free election, Eliot named three things that he thought a "university of liberal arts and sciences" should give its students. These were, first, "freedom in choice of studies"; second, "opportunity to win academic distinction in single subjects or special lines of study"; and third, "a discipline which distinctly imposes on each individual the responsibility of forming his own habits and guiding his own conduct."[4] At this distance of time, these goals seem in the abstract almost unexceptionable—notwithstanding the ambiguities of "free" choice. That is because, whereas McCosh may have won the debate as narrowly construed, the twentieth-century American university is fundamentally what Eliot wanted: a place where knowledge can expand indefinitely outward. And within a university constructed on these principles, he regarded the elective system not only as a desirable but as a logically necessary instrument of liberal education and social development. The virtue of his position is to have presented, with utter clarity, an extreme point of view, against which modifications have been worked ever since.

The third of Eliot's objectives is his starting point: no longer is the university or even the college, as in earlier years, to serve *in loco parentis*. Instead these institutions are training grounds in self-reliance. A university is best placed in or near a city like Rome, Paris, Vienna, or Berlin—in the presence of "a highly cultivated society." Oxford and Cambridge, both of them provincial and wedded to curricular prescription, are not in Eliot's exemplary list. In a great city, students "living in buildings whose doors stand open night and day, or in scattered lodging-houses cannot be mechanically protected from temptation." It is not the university's job to enforce rules of conduct, and none would be enforceable. Therefore, students have to "govern themselves."[5] The American institution now generally known as "student government" has some of its roots here, though it has become an odd hybrid, appealing to those who desire an office to run for more than to those few (if any) who may still want to stand disciplinary watch over their fellows. In any case, Eliot's argument for the curriculum begins in the ungovernability of students and then turns necessity into virtue. Self-reliance must extend to curricular choice—a natural extension of the university's social environment.

In addition, Eliot saw other considerations, which he called "mechanical," that were as constraining as those that put students beyond judicial reach. Yet the conclusions he drew from them are so exclusionary as to ask for explanation. Eliot's university (like that of John Henry Newman before him) is the locus of complete knowledge and thus endows the secular with a sacredness of its own, the sacredness of the universal. But complete knowledge lies beyond any individual's reach, and Eliot's argument from "mechanical" considerations assumes that the choice lies between requiring nothing and requiring everything, the latter being impossible. In a college with a prescribed curriculum, no more than 20 faculty are needed, as there had been at Harvard in the late 1860s. By the time Eliot debated McCosh, Harvard's faculty had grown to 80 (exclusive of laboratory assistants), who offered 425 hours of instruction each week, and on Eliot's calculation it would have taken 40 years for a student to "cover the present field," that is, to take every course offered—"and during those years the field would enlarge quite beyond his powers of occupation." Eliot's was a mind not disposed to compromise, hence his leap to the conclusion that election should be complete.[6]

As for a university itself, it "must try to teach every subject, above the grade of its admission requirements, for which there is any demand; and to teach it thoroughly enough to carry the advanced student to the confines of present knowledge, and make him capable of original research."[7] Neither Eliot nor Ezra Cornell, who founded his university with the same end in view, could have guessed at the logical extremes of a program that, like the free elective system itself, still haunts deliberations of the university about curricular decisions that encourage the differentiation and, hence, the proliferation of "cultures." Although the "rigorous limits which poverty imposes" prevent

Eliot's program from being realized, the standard on the far horizon matters more than the impossibility of reaching it.[8] Having inherited a job that once belonged to the monk in his cloister and to the church and that then was maintained by Enlightenment philosophers whose "heavenly city," as Carl Becker called it in the title of a famous book, was embodied in the fullness of encyclopedic compendia, the university collects the sum of all that can be known, thus keeping alive the dream of universal knowledge. In its very fragmentariness and in the complementary principle of free election lies its being, for in them lie both its universality and its moral conditions. The parts of the university sum up the corpus of knowledge. The impossibility of assimilating all knowledge imposes responsibilities of choice.

If that is the ideal, what is the secular reality? While Eliot preferred to think of his program as an education in moral choice, it is here that Darwinian, or Spencerian, habits of mind slip in. Eliot would have been unwise to launch his program under the banner of natural selection, even had he wanted to, yet Darwinism was bred into the bone of the academy during the 1870s. White, of Cornell, defended Darwin against his clerical opponents, and David Starr Jordan, of Stanford, described, as in a moment of reluctant conversion, "my acceptance of Darwinism" in the summer of 1873, contrary to the resistance of his teacher, Harvard's magisterial Louis Agassiz. To participate in the Darwinian and Spencerian revolution was the forward-looking thing to do, and Eliot did it. He had read Spencer's *Education: Intellectual, Moral, and Physical* (1861) and later visited Darwin on a trip to England in 1874. As a young scientist (like Jordan), Eliot would have come naturally to Darwinism—although as a New Englander, he also judged Darwinist social thought as restating Emersonian self-reliance in biological terms.[9] Furthermore, he knew Adam Smith, in whose *Wealth of Nations* he could have read Smith's praise of "the emulation which an unrestrained competition never fails to excite" and which serves as the best incentive to good instruction.[10] However sanctified the ideal university of Eliot's imagining, the reality implied a competitive, evolutionary model of knowledge. In the environment of free election, the fittest would survive best: the fittest students would succeed, the fittest teachers and the fittest courses would attract the best students, the fittest subjects would dominate the intellectual scene.

Eliot's presumption of this competitive environment stands out in his second proposition, that students should have the chance to win distinction "in single subjects or special lines of study." The set curriculum failed to distinguish between "the first scholar and the last," for each received the same diploma, and a university "cannot be developed on that plan." Rather, it should replicate conditions of the marketplace or of a natural world that itself resembles a competitive marketplace. Its inner drives are continuous striving and emulation, which lead students to make intellectual demands of the institution: "These honors encourage students to push far on single lines; whence arises a demand for advanced instruction in all departments in which honors can be won, and this demand, taken in connection with the competition which naturally springs up between different departments, stimulates the teachers, who in turn stimulate their pupils."[11] Students compete to win honors, "demanding" that departments provide advanced instruction. Departments compete to win students. Teachers, by implication, compete on behalf of their departments and for themselves. And, though Eliot never comes out and says so, universities compete, too. However genteel, it is warfare such as Herbert Spencer believed essential to the development of complex societies, warfare not of weaponry but of esteem. This model of the university has only grown stronger with time.

As early as 1911, Max Weber observed: "The American universities compete in a quite relentless way against their sister institutions. They bear the characteristics of competitive institutions. Like the modern industrial enterprise they pursue a policy of relentless selection with regard to proficiency, at least among their younger teachers." [12] Behind every ranking of departments or universities, behind mandatory student evaluations of teachers, behind the calls for excellence with which university leaders rally support, and behind certain of the resentments and jealousies that disfigure academic life, lie the values Eliot announced so clearly. Whatever he might have felt about required courses in Western civilization, he would have rejoiced in the desire for preeminence that marks the modern American university. And whatever compromises—compromises that he would have regarded as unwise, illiberal, and undemocratic— were to sully the purity of his elective system, he would have had the satisfaction of seeing his predictions in their elementary shape come true.

Describing his own experience, Eliot the scientist speaks a language of conversion that, though a Unitarian himself, he could be thought to have inherited from his more orthodox forebears. "I had," he reports, "experience as an undergraduate of a college course almost wholly required; for I happened upon nearly the lowest stage to which the elective system in Harvard College ever fell, after its initiation in 1825." After later service as a tutor and assistant professor under the system of prescription, he finally experienced six years' "separation" from Harvard, having failed to receive a further appointment. [13] He spent time in Europe, visiting England and settling down for stretches in Paris and Marburg, and eventually took up a faculty appointment at M.I.T. From there he returned to Harvard as its president, a very young man with something to prove to his elders. His six years' separation was Eliot's road to Damascus. During these years Eliot—like David Starr Jordan "accepting" Darwin—came to his faith in the world of competitive and secular forces on which Darwin and Spencer had set their seal. Yet whatever influence Darwin or Spencer may have had on Eliot's thinking, and however much he was troubled by the

ambiguities of race, he was too much the democrat ever to accept the neo-Darwinian and Anglo-Saxon "nativism" that dis-
figured American thinking in the late nineteenth century and
after.[14] Free election, as Eliot conceived it, was created in a
conjunction of intellectual forces with some conflicting implications that had not yet come sharply into focus.

Eliot's opponent in the debate of 1885 was a different figure
altogether. Born in Scotland and educated in Scottish universities, the terrible-tempered James McCosh had occupied the
chair of logic and metaphysics at Queen's College, Belfast, before coming to Princeton to be its president from 1868 to 1888.
He brought with him, in addition to his temper and bully-
ing ways, a considerable intellect, some commitment to new
forms of education combined with a steadfast Presbyterianism,
a belief in the importance of a coherent and in some degree
prescriptive liberal education, and a rhetorical flair that con-
trasted with Eliot's rather dry Unitarian manner. In the debate
McCosh played the preacher whose essential values have been
challenged.

In the free elective system, McCosh sees the shadow of
another secular revolution a century earlier, and he adopts from
Edmund Burke the combination of a strong personal voice and
a style of Olympian disappointment at seeing things so mis-
managed, especially (in this case) by one who had reason to
know better: "I am as much in favor of progress as President
Eliot, but I go on in a different, I believe a better way. I adopt
the new, I retain what is good in the old. I am disappointed, I
am grieved when I find another course pursued which allows,
which encourages, which tempts young men in their caprice to
choose easy subjects, and which are not fitted to enlarge or refine the mind, to produce scholars, or to send forth the great
body of the students as educated gentlemen." "Freedom," he
goes on, "freedom is the catch-word of this new departure. It is
a precious and an attractive word. But, O Liberty! what crimes
and cruelties have been perpetrated in thy name!"[15] McCosh

published his reply to Eliot under a chaste and seemly title, *The New Departure in College Education, Being a Reply to President Eliot's Defense of It in New York* (1885). He could as well have called it *Reflections on the Revolution in Cambridge.*

However impassioned, much of McCosh's argument runs along lines compatible with Eliot's own concern for intellectual vitality. McCosh worries that the caprice of young men will lead them to "easy" subjects—and in this anticipates the later complaints of Abraham Flexner, Robert Hutchins, and others about the insubstantiality of much in American higher education. Along with these reformers, McCosh would no doubt have been scandalized that in the 1950s, Harvard offered less academically inclined students a few famous courses such as "Boats" (Samuel Eliot Morison on naval history) or "Roman Law," said to have required little or no work to get a respectable grade. While Eliot claims that in a system of free election the fittest survive best, McCosh responds that by getting an intellectually cheap degree the not-so-fit can survive nicely. Here McCosh meets Eliot on his own ground.

Yet Eliot would have been, indeed was, unmoved. He believed that students have different talents and needs, that the easiness of a subject is hardly to be calculated, and that within the liberal arts subjects should be held in equal regard, just as (so he also believed) the varied cultures of American immigrants should be held in equal regard: "That all branches of sound knowledge are of equal dignity and equal educational value for mature students is the only hopeful and tenable view in our day." As for students who choose easy courses, regardless of subject, those "careless, indifferent, lazy boys who have no bent or intellectual ambition of any sort," Eliot asks, "what became of such boys under the uniform compulsory system?" He was indifferent to the likelihood that under either system the careless, the indifferent, and the lazy might not profit much: "it really does not make much difference what these unawakened minds dawdle with." Under the elective system, perhaps they will be aroused from their lethargy. If not, they will take courses that nonetheless offer "instruction on a higher plane than it can ever reach under a compulsory system." However unfit, the immature student becomes at least fitter under the elective system. Eliot would have made the point that hundreds of students at Harvard in the 1950s, perhaps thousands, emerged with at least a passing knowledge of maritime history and Roman law; and that a few (probably) went on to become maritime historians or scholars of ancient jurisprudence.[16]

But McCosh's quarrel lies above all with Eliot's vision of the university as a competitive marketplace. He affects contempt for the claim that "in a university the student must choose his studies and govern himself": "I saw at once that the question thus announced was large and loose, vague and ambiguous, plausible to the ear, but with no definite meaning. . . . The form is showy but I can expose it; I can prick the bubble so that all may know how little matter is inside." In place of the idea of the university as a free market, he endorsed Princeton's belief in a "Trinity of studies." The devout Presbyterian philosopher McCosh was not above a worldly-seeming allusion to Christian dogma, one that in its apparent worldliness conceals its true basis in religious feeling and a recognition that, in the new world of universities, underlying religious motives are most acceptable if recast in secular form.[17]

McCosh argues for what are now called "distribution requirements"—"branches which no candidate for the degree should be allowed to avoid." We would say students need some acquaintance with the several "fields" of knowledge. These metaphors, relying on an organic representation of the corpus of knowledge, themselves require a certain act of faith, for they pose taxonomic questions often suppressed in the interests of harmony—and whose arbitrariness is spotlighted by the prescribed trinity at Princeton, namely, language and literature, science, and philosophy: "Every educated man," says McCosh, "should know so much of one of these."[18] Eventually to be supplanted by the trinity of the humanities, social sciences, and natural sciences, the Princetonian trinity marks the construct-edness of such taxonomies. Yet almost any imaginable alternative to free election will rest on some such division, and the trinitarian structure has in its favor convenience (not too many categories, not too few) as well as its magical overtones. A Harvard committee in the 1960s that recommended replacing the triad of humanities, social sciences, and natural sciences with a twofold division was rebuffed.[19] That the triad is a trinity, like Princeton's or like the medieval trivium of grammar, rhetoric, and logic, yields its aura of the sacred.

The trouble with natural selection or democratic opportun-ism as an educational principle, in McCosh's view, was not only the principle of *laissez-faire* but the proliferation of difference itself. What could be more incomprehensible and intimidating than the Harvard catalogue, with its 200 offerings? "I confess," says McCosh ironically, to having "some difficulty" in under-standing it. "I would rather study the whole Cosmos. It [the Harvard catalogue] has a great many perplexities, which I can compare only to the cycles, epicycles, eccentricities of the old astronomy, so much more complex than that of Newton."[20] Once again, McCosh proves a clever debater. Under the veil of self-proclaimed modernity, he argues, Harvard's course offer-ings replicate an antiquated, Ptolemaic universe, full of impos-sibly complicated and obscure celestial relationships.

Against this proliferation McCosh proposes an ideal unity-in-diversity that he offers as scientific, Newtonian, up-to-date, and enlists on his side one of the most powerful of those who might be counted as the enemy, namely, Herbert Spencer: "In Nature, as Herbert Spencer has shown, there is differentia-tion which scatters, but there is also concentration which holds things together. There should be the same in higher educa-tion."[21] Here McCosh draws on the intellectual context that Eliot had prudently kept at arm's length. Even if Eliot had already won the war over the fundamental shape of the research university, McCosh can be said to have won this debate, judged not only by the popular response but by the almost universal triumph of "distribution requirements" in this century. Co-opting the enemy is good strategy.

If Spenser, the influential champion of *laissez-faire* economics based on individual interest, can be enrolled on the side of Princeton's trinity, the center may still hold. When McCosh pitched Spenser's authority against Eliot's in 1885, he and his audience would have had in mind events six years earlier, when Yale's conservative president, Noah Porter, had attempted to forbid William Graham Sumner, recently appointed to the chair of political and social science, from assigning Spencer's *Study of Sociology* to undergraduates. Sumner had replied that he would not give in "to a silly horror of Spencer's name."[22] Against the background of Spencerian or Darwinian thought, with all their challenge and allure, the nineteenth-century debate about higher education and its curriculum sharpens perceptibly. McCosh and Eliot were arguing about ways of seeing the world. And however much opposed in educational philosophy, each sought to offer in education what the church could no longer guarantee, namely, a secure grasp of what constituted the founding conditions of human knowledge.

McCosh's most fervent (and biblical) rhetoric arises from this recognition, vividly present in his peroration:

> Tell it not in Berlin or Oxford that the once most illustrious university in America no longer requires its graduates to know the most perfect language, the grandest literature, the most elevated thinking of all antiquity. Tell it not in Paris, tell it not in Cambridge in England, tell it not in Dublin, that Cambridge in America does not make mathematics obligatory on its students. Let not Edinburgh and Scotland and the Puritans in England know that a student may pass through the one Puritan College of America without having taken a single class of philosophy or a lesson in religion."[23]

McCosh defends liberal education as practiced at Oxford, where the classics were supreme, and at Cambridge, with its emphasis on mathematics; he defends religious learning by an association with philosophy and the traditions of liberal education; and he defends Princeton, Cambridge, and Oxford, provincial universities all, by grouping them with the urban centers of Berlin, Paris, and Edinburgh. The university, in McCosh's way of thinking, is not so much a particular place in a particular environment where students come to learn but an ideal state of mind, not just a training ground in self-reliance (which he might have granted)—and surely not a site of evolutionary struggle—but a manifestation of liberal community constructed around (for example) the "grandest literature" or the "most elevated thinking" of antiquity. In this, McCosh adopts the example not of his native Scotland but of Oxford and Cambridge, of Newman and Arnold.[24] In this, too—judged by subsequent attitudes and events in the American academy—he can be said largely to have won the debate.

III

Ancients, Moderns, and the Rise of Liberal Education

On one side of curricular arguments are usually the moderns, exponents of whatever they see as new and useful; on the other side are the ancients, exponents of the traditional and the true. "Ancients" and "moderns" take their names originally from the "battle of the books" fought in the late seventeenth and early eighteenth centuries between defenders of ancient literature and learning and defenders of, among other things, the new science. But there have always been ancients and moderns, and lines of allegiance may be generational as much as intellectual. If Western philosophy is a series of footnotes to Plato, the pedagogical debate of the past few years has been a series of footnotes to the several battles of the books that, in modern European history, began with Bacon's proposals for the "advancement of learning," his program for the overturning of Scholasticism and for an empirical conquest of the natural world. After Bacon came Locke, after Locke came Rousseau, after Rousseau came many others. It would be fruitless to attempt a complete genealogy of the moderns, even in the area of pedagogy, but when Eliot, who embodied the modern, debated McCosh, who combined a reverence for the old with a willingness (perhaps mostly strategic) to accommodate the new, they reenacted familiar dialogues as well as anticipating others to come.

Of course the division into ancients and moderns simplifies matters hugely. One champion of the eighteenth-century "moderns" was Richard Bentley (1662–1742), among the greatest of British classicists, whose achievements in philology (combined with his irascibility) made him the leader, in the minds of ancients like Swift and Pope, of those who diminished the values of ancient literature on behalf of the pedantic and the arcane. And McCosh, agile as he was, would surely have resisted being called an ancient. Yet allowing for imprecisions, certain arguments and attitudes mark each camp. Moderns want to sweep away worn-out knowledge and substitute knowledge that is more *useful*. They look ahead, sharing with John Dewey a belief that what is "alive and compelling" in education "moves toward some undiscovered future."[1] The ancients, looking to the past, have different criteria of usefulness. Where moderns often value technology, ancients value rational self-understanding. When moderns take their stand with Paine or Jefferson, ancients look to Burke. Ancients like to emphasize the etymology of "education" (from the Latin "educere," to "draw out") with its implication of processes by which mind and spirit perfect themselves. Ancients seldom have much use for the arcana of science or the products of technology: light bulbs or computers, however convenient, are helps to the understanding, useful in a modest way but not in the same way as Horace or Hegel. And science, at its most foolish or dangerous, can be worse than useless— the sort of thing Swift ridicules in *Gulliver's Travels*, in which some scientists try to extract sunbeams from cucumbers and to derive food from excrement while others think up engines of oppression and destruction.

Ancients perceive moderns, whatever their specific program, as subversive, both a threat and a symptom of whatever is wrong with the world as it has become. Moderns are lightning

rods for criticism because they seem to sum up the possibilities of error. Having laid out the path that has been mis-taken,
they may carry the burden for a long time. Because we are
heirs of the scientific revolution and of the Enlightenment,
ancients still hold Bacon, Locke, and Rousseau (though paradoxically they have been canonized) to account for bringing
the modern world into being. Bacon takes the blame for the
post-Renaissance triumph of the technological; a distinguished
scholar of Dante who taught at Harvard in the 1950s is said
to have ended his courses regularly by saying, "We must over-
come the Renaissance." Whatever his standing as the champion
of democratic individualism, Locke takes the blame for voca-
tional utilitarianism and for doubting the centrality of ancient
languages. And Rousseau's claim, in *Emile* (1762), that *Robinson Crusoe* was better preparation for life than Aristotle or even
Bacon, is only the least of the offenses that have convicted him,
as in Irving Babbitt's *Rousseau and Romanticism* (1919), of intellectual malfeasance and excess of every sort.

To be a modern is always to be concerned with education,
because it is on educational ground that battles of the books are
played out over time. Conversely, to be concerned with education and its curriculum means taking sides between ancients
and moderns or else trying to negotiate the territory between.
Conceiving their programs as requiring a radical revision of
educational practice, Bacon, Locke, and Rousseau set the terms
of the debate.

If these three reformers stand in the background of Eliot's
reform agenda, they do so at a distance. Of more immediate
influence are events and contests in nineteenth-century Britain,
a period of unprecedented attention to education, and at every
level. Here the familiar names are Newman and Arnold, for
what Newman had to say about universities or Arnold about
culture has become the habitual discourse of "liberal education," though with little attention to differences between them.
Yet Newman and Arnold, far from being radical ancients, came

at mid-stage of a process that established the doctrine of liberal education in certain of its modern acceptations, a process that included a full-scale battle of the books, as usual between ancients and moderns, after the turn of the nineteenth century.

Ancients generally occupy—or, as in the case of Swift, want to occupy—the center. Moderns more often exist or feel themselves as existing on the margins. In the curricular battle of the books waged at the start of the nineteenth century, Scotland and its enlightenment, represented by the always contentious *Edinburgh Review*, challenged the English universities, Oxford in particular, and elicited the response that helped fix in place certain important and surviving meanings of liberal education. Not all the champions of the *Edinburgh Review* were Scottish, but national as well as institutional loyalties were at stake, their presence emphasizing the persistent undertow of the political that pulls at the curricular debate. The creed of liberal education, as revised at Oxford in the early nineteenth century, was the ancients' inspired and adaptive response to insistent pressures of the modern. It was the creation of a particular time and place, an English invention maintained in the face of stiff opposition from the North.

In three reviews published in 1808 and 1809, the *Edinburgh Review* went on the attack. The first was by John Playfair, professor of natural philosophy at Edinburgh, on volumes of Laplace's *Celestial Mechanics* (1805); the second, by Richard Payne Knight on Thomas Falconer's edition of Strabo (1807); and the third, by Sydney Smith on Richard Lovell Edgeworth's *Essays on Professional Education* (1809). Playfair's review of Laplace attributed "the inferiority of the English mathematicians" to failures of "the two great centres from which knowledge is supposed to radiate over all the rest of the island" and to the particular failure of Oxford, "where the dictates of Aristotle are still listened to as infallible decrees." Knight's review of Falconer's Strabo—tendentiously labeled by the *Edinburgh Review* as "The Oxford Edition of Strabo" on grounds of its publication at the university press and Falconer's degree from Corpus Christi—commented, "Nothing in Europe is at all comparable, in point of extent and magnificence, to the endowment of the University of Oxford,—or to the veneration which is there paid to the Greek and Latin languages." Then Knight criticized the want of classical scholarship coming out of Oxford and, as in the edition at hand, the faultiness of that which did. Finally, Smith's review of Edgeworth, a considerable figure in the educational reform movement who in 1771 had shown his son to Rousseau as a model of an education on Rousseau's principles, echoed Edgeworth on the misguided reverence for classical learning in England, where education "trains up many young men in a style of elegant imbecility" and produces, at Oxford, "a delusive sort of splendour." English education, according to the *Edinburgh Review*, did the wrong thing and did it badly.[2]

About the origins of "liberal education" in its current acceptation no great clarity exists, but the statutory introduction of public examinations at Oxford at the turn of the century had changed the educational landscape, and it was this new Oxford, with its emphasis on *literae humaniores*, that drew the fire of the *Edinburgh Review*.[3] One reason behind the statute of 1800—though in the opinion of Sheldon Rothblatt, not the main one—was persistent criticism of Oxford in the eighteenth century, most famously by Edward Gibbon, as a sleeping place for its dons. A more substantial reason, Rothblatt believes, was "generational" and "cultural" change, some of it reflected in dangerous intellectual tendencies among the students. Since "free-thinking among the elite youth of the kingdom was unsettling to the social peace," the rigor of the new examinations, which required acquaintance with "the Elements of Religion, and the Doctrinal Articles" as well as with classical texts, was calculated "to absorb student interest and, if possible, deflect it from subjects and activities more immediately threatening to the surviving *ancien régime* in England."[4] Though difficult to test, this hypothesis ascribes a political overlay to a modern version of liberal education from its point of origin. No longer simply the education of a gentleman, liberal education in this hypothesis takes on a diversionary function, like the tub (allegorized by Swift) said to have been thrown out by seamen to divert a whale from attacking a ship (in Swift's hands, the ship of state). But such a function could not stand much exposure to the light and in Oxford's response to the *Edinburgh Review* could be voiced only by indirection. What Oxford had to do was outspokenly to defend the new rigor of its classical curriculum on strictly educational grounds; and, in doing so, to refine those principles on which the curriculum was officially based.

The task fell to its professor of poetry Edward Copleston, a graduate of Corpus Christi, a fellow and later provost of Oriel, and a capable Latinist. He had already published a witty parody of the *Edinburgh Review* called *Advice to a Young Reviewer, with a Specimen of the Art* (1807), his "specimen of the art" being a "review" of Milton's *L'Allegro*: "Upon the whole, Mr. Milton seems to be possessed of some fancy and talent for rhyming . . . , but it is not all the Zephyrs, and Auroras, and Corydons, and Thyrsis's, aye, not his junketing Queen Mab, and drudging Goblins, that will ever make him a Poet."[5] Copleston was therefore a natural for the more demanding job that now had to be done, and his *Reply to the Calumnies of the "Edinburgh Review" Against Oxford* (1810), to which he later added two more "replies," inspired the *Review* to 30 pages of fierce rhetoric. Vividly displaying the confrontation of upstart Scot and high-minded albeit very contentious Oxonian, the controversy set a typical insurgent modernism against an equally typical ancient piety.

Also typical, the combat was one of style as well as substance, with the *Edinburgh Review* lampooning Copleston's rhetoric as overblown fustian and ruthlessly lifting from context this sample:

> There are emotions which eloquence can raise, and which
> lead to loftier thoughts and nobler aspirings than commonly
> spring up in the private intercourse of men: when the latent

flame of genius has been kindled by some transient ray, shot
perhaps at random, and aimed least where it took the greatest effect, but which has set all the kindred sparks that lay
there, in such a heat and stir, as that no torpid indolence,
or low earthy-rooted cares, shall ever again smother or keep
them down. From this high lineage may spring a never-failing
race; few indeed, but more illustrious because they are few,
through whom the royal blood of philosophy shall descend.[6]

Detached from its setting, this seems to celebrate classical eloquence but is in fact a criticism of lectures, which is to say
the Scottish method, as an education only for an attentive few
in contrast to Oxford's more egalitarian tutorials. Very likely
Copleston has in mind the lectures of Dugald Stewart, Edinburgh's professor of moral philosophy, whose oratory was so
memorable, despite an "asthmatic" tendency to clear his throat,
that it was said of him, "there was eloquence in his very spit-
ting."[7] Perhaps Copleston is even exercising his talent for parody. But the *Review*, intent on exposing the Coplestonian, and
Oxonian, manner as falsely sublime, seizes the occasion:

> He who has seen a barn-door fowl flying—and only he—can
> form some conception of this tutor's eloquence. With his neck
> and hinder parts brought into a line,—with loud screams,
> and all the agony of feather'd fatness,—the ponderous little
> glutton flaps himself up into the air, and, soaring four feet
> above the level of our earth, falls dull and breathless on his
> native dunghill.[8]

Moderns are down-to-earth, realistic; ancients fall into bathos.
That is the message of the *Review*, and even those friendly
to Oxford might concede that some points have been scored.
The "agony of feather'd fatness," an endemic consequence
of preacherly self-defensiveness (Copleston later was bishop of
Llandaff), sometimes undermines the best rhetorical efforts of
the ancients.

The rhetorical coloring of Copleston's defense gives some

support to Rothblatt's hypothesis, for the *Reply* communicates a sense of dangers at hand greater than any Copleston cares to name. What Oxford aims to produce is not just "men . . . whose minds are imbued with literature according to their several measures of capacity" but men "impressed with what we hold to be the soundest principles of policy and religion"— impressed with these religious principles, it should be remembered, by public examination.[9] Yet in one sense nothing is new about this goal, and the urgency of Copleston's liberal piety is therefore hard to gauge. What *is* new, important, and demonstrable is his version of a liberal education in the classics as a poultice for the deep, twin wounds of commercialism and professionalization, an argument that has survived and flourished in the commercial and professional setting of the modern university, where liberal education is looked upon as a way of staying human in a world of inhuman practices. Liberal education, that is, helps save us from our worst selves by establishing a social bond.

Among those who stand to benefit most from a liberal education Copleston names surgeons and generals, thus ensuring a wide application of his principle—and perhaps responding to Edgeworth's *Essays on Professional Education*, in particular the chapter "On Military and Naval Education," where Edgeworth, having in mind Nelson's loss of an arm, had said: "As to the actual value of the accomplishment of understanding Greek or even Latin, it might perhaps be more useful for a soldier to have learnt to write readily with either hand, than to be able to write Latin elegantly." Surgeons and generals may in the course of their profession need sometimes to "dismiss the common feelings of human nature," Copleston concedes; but "when the emergency is past," society requires "some other contribution from each individual, besides the particular duties of his profession." A "liberal intercourse" must be established; if not, "it is the common failing of human nature, to be engrossed with petty views and interests, to under-rate the importance of all in which we are not concerned, to carry our partial notions into cases where they are inapplicable, to act, in short, as so many unconnected units, displacing and repelling one another."[10]

And where can the solidarity of an organic culture be found if not in "the cultivation of literature"—that is, classical literature—"which, among the higher and middle departments of life, unites the jarring sects and subdivisions in one interest, which supplies common topics, and kindles common feelings, unmixed with those common prejudices with which all professions are more or less infected?" Great and ancient books and the training needed to understand them provide a "complete and generous education" that imparts "a dignity to the several professions of life, and to mercantile adventure." Should he ever listen in to current faculty debates from the security of the grave, Copleston might take some wry satisfaction in learning that this version of liberal education has had so much staying power in an ever more professional and mercantile environment. What has changed most is the content, not the concept, of liberal education, now become an ample vessel into which any number of saving remedies may be poured.[11]

When the battle between the moderns of Scotland and the ancients of Oxford broke out again two decades later, it did not this time set defenders of scholarship, science or practicality against defenders of liberal education. Instead the issue was the content of liberal education itself. On the Scottish side was Sir William Hamilton, professor of civil history at the University of Edinburgh and, earlier, a worthy but disappointed candidate for Edinburgh's chair of moral philosophy. Editorship of the *Edinburgh Review* having passed to Macvey Napier from the intemperately witty Francis Jeffrey in 1828, Hamilton became a regular contributor, publishing an article in June 1831, "On the State of the English Universities, with More Especial Reference to Oxford," and then a response in December to the inevitable Oxonian reply, this one written by another Oriel graduate, Vaughan Thomas, and entitled *The Legality of the Present Academical System of the University of Oxford Asserted*

Against the New Calumnies of the "Edinburgh Review". To these pieces, Hamilton later added a long appendix, "On a Reform of the English Universities, with Especial Reference to Oxford; and Limited to the Faculty of Arts"; all of these were collected in *Discussions on Philosophy and Literature, Education and University Reform* (1852). A former holder of a fellowship for Scottish students at Balliol with claims, therefore, to being an insider, Hamilton struck a judicious note in his first article, in keeping with the less strident habits of the new *Edinburgh Review*. His response to Thomas was not so measured, but in the later appendix Hamilton avoids slash-and-burn. He was an opponent to be reckoned with, especially so because he accepted the premises of liberal education, indeed helped increase their currency.

Hamilton believed that Oxford's individual colleges had illegally usurped the authority of the university, with unhappy results. Without effective oversight at the university level, control over instruction diminishes and teaching languishes in the hands of the incompetent. Worse yet, competition between students falters: "The old system daily collected into large classes, under the same professor, the whole youth of the University of equal standing, and thus rendered possible a keen and constant and unremitted competition; the new, which elevates the colleges and halls into so many little universities, and in these houses distributes the students, without regard to ability or standing, among some fifty tutors, frustrates all emulation among the members of its small and ill-assorted classes."[12] Despite the advent of honors examinations at the beginning of the century, which slowly became the norm after the statute of 1800, the power of colleges dulls "emulation." So does the tutorial system, whereas lectures stimulate it. Whatever reforms have been effected, still others are needed. These arguments Hamilton restated in answering Thomas. Then in his more deliberate appendix of 1852 he put the question, in what should liberal education in a university consist?

Hamilton's answer—namely, philosophy—reflected not only

his own vocation but a basic conflict between the Scottish Enlightenment and English classicism. What matters to Hamilton
is not philosophy as history but philosophy as the road to ethical
understanding and as an epistemological prerequisite to secular
knowledge. In this, he anticipates those who these days value
"method" and "interpretation" more than history or who, it
might better be said, value method and interpretation as prerequisite to historical and other forms of knowledge. Hamilton
is very "modern"—even granting that versions of his argument
are everywhere to be found in antiquity, when (after all) there
were no ancients to look back to.

In advancing his claims, Hamilton took up where the *Edinburgh Review* had left off 40 years before, the *Review* having
criticized Oxford's neglect of moral philosophy, and Copleston
having answered that ethics were incorporated in the teachings
of religion. To the *Review*, standing for modern enlightenment,
Copleston's position was rank obscurantism. In the last paragraph of its answer to Copleston's *Reply*, the *Review* gives a final
wave of the hand, calculated and dismissive: "We had almost
forgotten to state, that this author's substitutes for lectures in
moral philosophy, are sermons delivered from the University
pulpit. He appears totally ignorant of what the terms *moral
philosophy* mean. But enough of him and his ignorance." [13] In
this sequel, however, Hamilton sidesteps the religious question
by emphasizing the epistemological content of philosophical
understanding.

Once the value of "liberal education" is assumed, it comes
next to ask whether the job is to provide a corpus of knowledge or a means of knowing, granting that a corpus of knowledge may teach method by experience and example while
attention to method can hardly take place in the absence of example. Hamilton is clear and outspoken about this. Split up
into separate colleges and almost exclusively devoted to classical learning, Oxford "now abandons both Philosophy itself
and the philosophical treatment of what it professes to teach."

In fact Oxford's ancients have abandoned the *real* tradition of the ancients, which Hamilton in his modernity merely wishes to recapture. As "the science of science—the theory of what we *can* know and think and do, in a word,—the knowledge of ourselves," philosophy is the true "object of liberal education, at once of paramount importance in itself, and the requisite condition of every other liberal science." Though specializing in philology, the English do it badly because they fail to do it "philosophically." Had they learned from the parallel examples of Kant and his fellow student at Königsberg, the classicist David Ruhnken, they would have realized that philology and philosophy reinforce each other: "The genius of each seemed then . . . strongly to incline towards the studies in which the other afterwards reigned paramount. And truly, the best pro-gymnastic of philosophy is the theory of language; and how necessary is philosophy and the practice of speculation to any progress of account in the higher philology, Ruhnken himself has authoritatively declared." To put Hamilton's argument in contemporary terms again, this might be translated without serious distortion into the proposition that "theory" should be at the heart of literary study. Hamilton's dispute with Oxford's canonical version of liberal education is still reenacted regularly.[14]

If prescriptions like Hamilton's or those of literary theorists have proven hard to administer, that is not because they are not well thought out but because they are utopian. Not everyone has an aptitude for the abstruse. At the same time, something like Hamilton's proposition lies behind the surviving, often-articulated claim that "critical thinking" is what liberal education is all about, a claim that, taken seriously, could mitigate territorial skirmishes about the content of what should be taught. It is also a claim independently dear to those in the university who teach or concern themselves with introductory courses in writing. Under the protection of "writing," "critical thinking" and even approximations of formal logic have found shelter. To the extent that "writing" has become philosophy for the many, Hamilton's arguments in deflected form have had some staying power.

The third major episode in this battle of the books, the last before Newman and Arnold appeared dominantly on the scene, occurred in 1845. It involved science more than literature and Cambridge more than Oxford, took its origin in the contrasting habits of American and English universities, and could be called a skirmish between Scottish and English interests only by an accident of birth and in its revival of concerns that the *Edinburgh Review* had raised earlier in the century. The combatants were the geologist Charles Lyell, born in Scotland but taken to England at the age of one and educated at Exeter College, Oxford, whose two-volume *Travels in North America*—the journal of a trip he made in 1841–42—appeared in the summer of 1845; and, on the other side, the polymath philosopher, scientist, mathematician, and master of Trinity College, Cambridge, William Whewell, whose *Of a Liberal Education in General* appeared in autumn of the same year, much of it reiterating arguments in his *Thoughts on the Study of Mathematics, as a Part of a Liberal Education* (1835) and *On the Principles of English University Education* (1837). On his travels Lyell had become familiar with American higher education, especially at Harvard, and whatever Charles Eliot's retrospective opinion of Harvard's curriculum in the 1840s, Lyell found the contrast with English universities to Harvard's advantage. At the same time, although his interests lay chiefly in the advancement of scientific learning, he had to confront—and did so ingeniously— the increasingly powerful claim on the public mind of liberal education as practiced in the English universities.

As Whewell protested, the title of Lyell's volumes, *Travels in North America; with Geological Observations on the United States, Canada, and Nova Scotia*, gave no hint that they would contain, at the close of volume one, adjacent to geological observations about the Gay Head cliffs on Martha's Vineyard, a chapter devoted to the "peculiarities" of English universities and to possible "remedies and reforms." After visiting Martha's Vineyard, Lyell went to Boston for the annual meeting of the Association of American Geologists, and his observations on English and American education arise from this experience.[15]

"In no subject," Lyell says, "do the Americans display more earnestness than in their desire to improve their system of education, both elementary and academical." At Harvard, professors are "each assisted by one or more tutors," many are "well known in the literary world as authors," only five (Lyell is evidently glad to report) "were educated for the pulpit," and "the proportion of professors to students . . . is far greater than that of college tutors in the English universities." Against this background, Lyell reports—as it were, dutifully—awkward questions put to him about the English universities: "Every inquiry into the present state of the universities in America drew forth from my informants, in return, many questions respecting Oxford and Cambridge. I was asked by professors of geology, chemistry, modern history, modern literature, and other branches of knowledge, why the classes for these subjects had recently fallen off in the English universities?" Was it (perhaps) the consequence of the religious reaffirmations of Newman's Tractarian movement?[16]

Under the spell of his North American experience, Lyell offers a miniature history of English higher education, stressing the limiting effects of the compulsory examinations and disputing "the boast of writers who extol our university system above that of other countries, that we promote *liberal* studies, and do not condescend to qualify students for a lucrative profession or trade." To this Lyell answers cleverly that, on the contrary, English education is not liberal enough. Of the students who "toil at" Latin, Greek, and (at Cambridge) mathematics, most do so in order to make a future livelihood as tutors or schoolmasters. Why then should not "the utilitarianism of our universities comprehend equally, within the sphere of its educational training, those branches of general knowledge which are equally essential to the future statesman, divine, lawyer, physician, and men of other liberal callings?" It is an adroit argument, relying on the elasticity of the liberal ideal. Though it is not daring to describe government, law, or medicine as liberal callings, exponents of liberal education as practiced at Oxford and Cambridge could not well have accepted Lyell's elision of the difference between a liberal education and a liberal calling or ignored the threat thus posed to a more homogeneous ideal of liberal education by the sheer number of liberal callings.[17]

In his next paragraph, Lyell looks ahead to a "professorial plan of instruction" in the English universities under which tutors "would divide themselves at once into as many sections as there are departments of study recognised in the public examinations. They would devote their minds steadily to subjects connected with theology, or with law, or medicine, or engineering, or literary criticism, or applied mathematics, or other branches."[18] It is a vision of the modern, specialized, departmentalized university, a vision perhaps influenced by Lyell's acquaintance with Harvard's George Ticknor, a professor of literature and a reformer whose proposals, though unsuccessful in the 1820s, bore fruit in the administration of his nephew Charles Eliot.[19] It comes as no surprise that young Eliot, just arrived in England in 1863, six years before he took up his presidency at Harvard, eagerly sought out Lyell's acquaintance.[20] Like Lyell, Eliot was to accept the legitimacy of liberal education while redefining it in a way that in the eyes of some seemed to shake its foundations.

Under the scheme of compulsory examinations, Lyell reports, sciences have languished in English universities. "Three-fourths of the sciences, still nominally taught at Oxford, . . . have been virtually exiled from the University." Classrooms of chemistry, botany, geometry, astronomy, "experimental philosophy," and other of the "exiled" fields, even ancient history and poetry, are nearly deserted. Nor are things better at Cambridge, where mathematics are more central: "All branches of knowledge taught by the professors—in a word, every subject except what is understood in our universities by classics and mathematics—have had sentence of banishment passed upon them." As for Whewell's vindication of classics and mathematics, Lyell asks whether it should not be "one of our chief objects" to prepare the student "to form sound opinions in matters connected with moral, political, or physical science?" And to the question, why are the best modern editions of Greek and Latin authors not usually the product of English scholarship, he answers by praising specialization: "The highest excellence in literature or in science can only result from a life perseveringly devoted to one department. Such unity of purpose and concentration of power is wholly inconsistent with our academical machinery of tuition." Lyell was a prophet of the modern research university.[21]

Tucked away in a corner of *Travels in North America*, Lyell's remarks have largely escaped notice, but they did not escape William Whewell, who, having "accidentally stumbled" on them, expressed his surprise at finding them "in a work so popular in its form and matter, and giving in its title so little warning of its controversial character." Arguing for a less constricted curriculum, Lyell had said, "No one who is master of his favourite science will fail to inspire the minds of his more intellectual scholars with a love of what he teaches, and a regard and admiration for their instructor." Resorting to the ritual of an academic *reductio ad absurdum*, Whewell jokes at Lyell: "This is, I think, highly probable. I am so far from doubting it, that I believe it to be true of subjects in which the supposed science is altogether empty and fallacious. I believe that not only a philosophical and eloquent lecturer on Geology or Chemistry, but that an ingenious and enthusiastic lecturer on Craniology, or Animal Magnetism, will generally inspire a large portion of his audience with such feelings." Then Whewell recurs to the Coplestonian theme of liberal education as schooling for the

many, not just the few: "But I do not think anything worthy to
be called a Liberal Education could be carried on by the operation of personal character and influence of this kind. To educate
young men, we must direct the general course of the studies
of all, and not merely excite the admiration and enthusiasm of
a few." There is no need to track Whewell's response, by now
familiar in its tendencies, any further.[22]

At this point, Newman and Arnold enter the scene. It was
their mission to carry the idea of liberal education to the world
beyond the university. They were not, however, of a single
mind. Representing two distinct strains of humanism, their
views—especially Arnold's—became part of a belief system
that has sometimes tugged against itself. With them, separate
currents of thought flow into the main stream. As the two currents merge, there comes the need to locate the original ground
of difference, for it still defines alternative attitudes to the moral
design of liberal education. Those who continue to think of
themselves as in some sense traditional humanists might be divided into "Arnoldians" and "Newmanians." Bringing the distinction more into view will better discriminate attitudes that
are sometimes supposed to be the same.

IV

Two Strains of Humanism

'The Idea of a University' and 'Culture and Anarchy'

The changes that marked the first half of the nineteenth century in England became a flood in 1850. For at least twenty years, committees abounded and legislation flourished.[1] Out of all this activity, and out of the battle of the books that saw Oxford defending its curriculum, came Newman's *The Idea of a University* and Arnold's *Culture and Anarchy*. Despite their sense of embattlement, Newman and Arnold construct their edifice on foundations that Oxford had already laid. As provost of Oriel, Edward Copleston had treated the reticent young Newman kindly when he won his fellowship there in 1822; and though the relationship between them was not always harmonious, Newman commemorates Copleston in *The Idea of a University*.[2] And Arnold, himself a graduate of Balliol, elected a fellow of Oriel in 1847, and Oxford's professor of poetry from 1857 to 1867, in *Culture and Anarchy* credited Newman's Oxford movement with the "keen desire for beauty and sweetness" that helped undermine "the self-confident Liberalism of the last thirty years"— credited it with a program, that is, that matched Arnold's own: "It is in this manner that the sentiment of Oxford for beauty and sweetness conquers, and in this manner long may it continue to conquer!"[3] Notwithstanding the differences between New-man's humanism and Arnold's, both drew from a storehouse of ideas and sentiments that Oxford had supplied.

The Idea of a University and *Culture and Anarchy* each arose in occasions of the moment. Each is a gathering of related materials, not a single discourse. Each was vastly popular. And each raises the question, driven by cultural change and increasingly troublesome, of the relationship between religion and secular learning. What would be for Eliot and McCosh a strong undertow had for Newman and Arnold to be confronted more directly. The modern idea of "liberal education" having been set in place and university education no longer serving as, predominantly, training for a clerical vocation, believers confronted the growing chasm between the claims of the divine and the claims of the human in the area of learning. And although both strove to heal or to deny the rift, thus distinguishing themselves from Eliot, who took it as a given, Newman and Arnold ultimately enhanced the legitimacy of learning as a secular activity, sanctioning its characteristic language of justification and providing it with a religiosity all its own. McCosh's reference to Princeton's trinity of studies was but one (slightly surprising) example of how the rhetorical winds were about to blow.

The Idea of a University includes, first, a series of lectures that Newman, just designated president of the newly created Catholic University of Ireland, delivered in 1852 with the hope of persuading Dubliners to support the undertaking; and, second, a group of lectures and essays addressed to the University community during the 1850s. The first series was printed weekly as the lectures were delivered, then collected in 1852 as *Discourses on University Education Addressed to the Catholics of Dublin*, and finally revised for republication in 1859. Separately published in 1859 were *Lectures and Essays on University Subjects*. In 1873 the *Discourses* and the *Lectures* were finally combined as *The Idea of a University*, then reissued in six more editions before Newman's death, in 1890. Not until the success of Bloom's *The Closing of the American Mind* would a volume on higher education achieve such visibility.

Now more than in Newman's day, universities justify and defend themselves to multiple constituencies, each with a different agenda: trustees with fiduciary responsibilities; faculty who see themselves not as employees but as autonomous custodians of the university's welfare; undergraduates for whom the local and immediate count most; graduate students intent on their professional futures; alumni blessed or burdened by the memory of how things used to be; politicians of every hue; federal bureaucrats; and "the public." These different constituencies not only find different meanings in liberal education but, in the pulling between them, exercise a shaping power upon it. The situation Newman faced in 1852 was similar. As president-designate of the Catholic University, he had violently competing interests to take into account as well as conflicting values within himself. In the dexterity of his response, at least to his external constituencies, he established a style that has become second nature, a basic survival mechanism, for many who find themselves speaking for the universities.

The new university had been a matter of controversy, within and without the Catholic establishment, ever since Sir Robert Peel proposed in 1845 a secular, nondenominational university in Ireland that would admit Catholics. The archbishop of Dublin favored the plan, while Rome preferred a specifically Catholic university instead. With support from a new archbishop, Rome prevailed, and in this context Newman was asked to deliver his lectures. In them he had to appeal to supporters, to those who had favored Peel's scheme, and, as a London-born graduate of Oxford, to nationalists who feared that a university would be inimical to Irish interests.[4] Not surprisingly, the task gave him great difficulty, and nowhere more so than in his account of reasons for studying the secular literature on which Oxford's liberal education was grounded.

Everywhere central to Newman's exposition is the delicate

balance between authority and knowledge. For him, authority means the Roman church, yet his dilemma differs little from that of secular humanists who have to weigh the balance between social authority and the subversive potency of canonical texts. The value of knowledge for its own sake has somehow to be set aside from, yet not be seen as destructive of, the claims of providence or the state. To that end, the argument runs that secular knowledge may flower into secular morality not hostile to authority and, at best, that it readies the mind for truths of the divine order or of the social structure within which it finds expression. On this account, knowledge occupies a unique space, though not an autonomous existence, within the context of the religious or the social. Liberal education treats of value, and an education in value may—though it need not—lead on to virtue. Unlike the Enlightenment's valorizing of the subversive and the heretical, liberal education in this account is a halfway house, a stage of the pilgrim's progress in which vital inclinations of the mind are directed, trained, and satisfied.

But it is *not* a training in virtue, and it is this belief of the Catholic Newman's that crucially distinguishes him from Arnold, from Arnold's disciples, and from many who, though opposed to Arnold's version of high culture, nonetheless believe as much as he that liberal education provides training in how to lead a good life. In Roger Kimball's *Tenured Radicals* (1990), one of the numerous recent salvos aimed at the academy, Arnold is mentioned warmly and often, Newman not once. To Arnold, Kimball attributes the proposition, which he finds praiseworthy, that the intellectual *telos* of culture is truth and the moral *telos* of culture, virtue. He also quotes Barbara Johnson, characterized as a "champion of radical feminism" and therefore *not* praiseworthy, as having said at a symposium, "Professors should have less freedom of expression than writers and artists, because professors are supposed to be creating a better world."[5] Whether Kimball represents Johnson's spoken words accurately there is no telling, but both Kimball and Arnold share with Johnson, on Kimball's own account, the pedagogical agenda of creating a better world, and the dispute—the only dispute, one might say—is how to do it. For Kimball and Arnold, it is a matter of training individuals up to virtue; for Johnson, of remaking social convention. Any such agenda Newman rejects.

The end of liberal education, in Newman's account, is not "to make men better": "This I will not for an instant allow." Or again, "Knowledge is one thing, virtue is another." "However enlightened, however profound," secular philosophy "gives no command over the passions, no influential motives, no vivifying principles." And, in one of the eloquent moments that make reading Newman exhilarating: "Quarry the granite rock with razors, or moor the vessel with a thread of silk; then may you hope with such keen and delicate instruments as human knowledge and human reason to contend against those giants, the passion and the pride of man." Liberal education, then, makes neither a Christian nor a Catholic. What it does, and here Newman speaks like more the traditionalist than he really was, is to make "the gentleman."⁶

This liberally educated gentleman, to be sure, is not just the cultivated proprietor of landed estates. He is an eighteenth-century benevolist. In Newman's famous description, "It is almost a definition of a gentleman to say he is one who never inflicts pain." There follows a catalogue of what many, less scrupulous than Newman, would call gentlemanly "virtues": compassion, prudence, patience, forbearance, courtesy, consideration, toleration, and so on. Yet as an apostle of the comfortable, this more or less traditional gentleman is faintly risible, a figure from whose portrait one can predict our own discomfort with the merely comfortable and "gentlemanly": "His benefits may be considered as parallel to what are called comforts or conveniences in arrangements of a personal nature: like an easy chair or a good fire, which do their part in dispelling cold and fatigue, though nature provides both means of rest and animal

heat without them."[7] If Newman's defense of liberal education
mounted no higher, *The Idea of a University* would seem parochial, the mere concession of a devout Catholic to the habits of
the world. So in a sense it is, but Newman can rise above gentle-
manliness, as he does when the going is toughest and he confronts uncompromising conflicts of value. In his final lecture,
"Duties of the Church to Knowledge," he reaches that most
sensitive of subjects, the teaching of literature in a Catholic university—or, to generalize, the teaching of material potentially
offensive to religion or the social order. Newman's defense, unlike Arnold's, is that literature affords an education for and in a
fallen world.

And that is an education steeped in awareness of sin: "It
is a contradiction in terms to attempt a sinless Literature of
sinful man." Though "sin" is no longer a common feature on
the strategic maps of curricular warriors, Newman's percep-
tion of human frailty and his consequent valuing of "generosity
of spirit," "liberality of sentiment," and "kindness of heart"—
qualities he attributes to his predecessor Copleston—lie almost
surreptitiously near the center of some surviving brands of
humanism. Secular learning and literature serve as compen-
satory instruments, then, as they do in Copleston's account,
though less extensively there. What was for Copleston the
means of not losing sight of the human, whether one was
a surgeon or a general, is for Newman a means of coming
to understand the worldliness of the world. Those who have
been educated to the fact of frailty share a knowledge essentially religious, although Newman does not say so, namely, the
knowledge that all have sinned. Imaginative literature prepares
the student, and this Newman does say, "to swim in troubled
waters."[8]

Newman is a great writer. He thinks in long breaths, and the
sonorities of his prose match the strength of his thought. He
also speaks eloquently for some, by no means the most outspoken of humanists, who profess no faith other than that of

learning, who might best be called believers *manqués*, and who yield little to Newman in their hard judgment of the ways of the world, even including in the long run the ways of learning itself. In a lengthy excursus of great power and beauty, which it would be a pity to abridge, Newman challenges those who want to proscribe secular literature and, with it, preparation for swimming in the troubled waters of the world:

If then a University is a direct preparation for this world, let it be what it professes. It is not a Convent, it is not a Seminary; it is a place to fit men of the world for the world. We cannot possibly keep them from plunging into the world, with all its ways and principles and maxims, when their time comes; but we can prepare them against what is inevitable; and it is not the way to learn to swim in troubled waters, never to have gone into them. Proscribe (I do not merely say particular authors, particular works, particular passages) but Secular Literature as such; cut out from your class books all broad manifestations of the natural man; and those manifestations are waiting for your pupil's benefit at the very doors of your lecture room in living and breathing substance. They will meet him there in all the charm of novelty, and all the fascination of genius or of amiableness. To-day a pupil, to-morrow a member of the great world: to-day confined to the Lives of the Saints, to-morrow thrown upon Babel;—thrown on Babel, without the honest indulgence of wit and humour and imagination having ever been permitted to him, without any fastidiousness of taste wrought into him, without any rule given him for discriminating "the precious from the vile," beauty from sin, the truth from the sophistry of nature, what is innocent from what is poison. You have refused him the masters of human thought, who would in some sense have educated him, because of their incidental corruption: you have shut up from him those whose thoughts strike home to our hearts, whose words are proverbs, whose names are indigenous to all the world, who are the standard of their mother tongue, and the pride and boast of their country-

men, Homer, Ariosto, Cervantes, Shakespeare, because the
old Adam smelt rank in them; and for what have you reserved
him? You have given him "a liberty unto" the multitudinous
blasphemy of his day; you have made him free of its newspapers, its reviews, its magazines, its novels, its controversial
pamphlets, of its Parliamentary debates, its law proceedings,
its platform speeches, its songs, its drama, its theatre, of its
enveloping, stifling atmosphere of death. You have succeeded
but in this,—in making the world his University.[9]

"Newmanians" regret the corruption of the world and regard
literature, which participates inescapably if incidentally in that
corruption, as palliative; "Arnoldians," different in mood as
well as in belief, celebrate "the great tradition" as the way to
set things right. At present, Arnoldians like Roger Kimball are
in the ascendant, at least in their high visibility. But if those
who call themselves humanists were somehow to be polled,
the ranks of Newmanian believers *manqués* would turn out (I
think) to be larger than their collective quietness might lead
anyone to suppose. The number of faculty who actually participate in the hurly-burly of curricular debates is not so large
as the visibility of these debates seems to imply. Some faculty
share a natural human reticence and consequently shun public
roles. Some also share with Newman a skepticism about the
claims of literature and human learning to transcendent value.

If Arnold's esteem for "culture," which he regards as the
source of what Swift called the "noblest" things, sweetness
and light—unlike Newman's sense of the sinfulness lying at
the heart of secular literature—has become a rallying call in
America, that is what he would have liked. Nostalgic for the
medieval Oxford of Gothic spires, hopeful of an England har-
moniously united under the double establishment of church
and culture, but in his more practical role of government bu-
reaucrat a student of education abroad, Arnold addressed *Culture and Anarchy* (1869; revised, 1875) almost as much to his
American as to his English readers. The United States plays a

large part in Arnold's thought and experience. As early as 1853, while reading Margaret Fuller, he lamented to Arthur Hugh Clough "the absence of men of any culture in America" which "must have made her run so wildly, and for many years made her insufferable." [10] In the 1880s, on two lecture tours to the United States, he brought the religion of culture to the American outback, and in 1888, the year of his death, he published an essay to demonstrate this nation's lack of "distinction" and "beauty." [11] And in the Preface to *Culture and Anarchy*, America stands for much of what Arnold hopes to amend. The reward for this drumroll of criticism was that, though he was at first regarded in this country as a "supercilious fop," Arnold soon became a "godly figure." [12] American humanism in this century has sought to blunt the edge of his criticism by putting his remedies into effect.

As a laboratory of social and educational experiment, America has always provided examples to be imitated or avoided. In the course of his cautionary advice, Arnold misquotes the Quaker reformer John Bright: "I believe the people of the United States have offered to the world more valuable information during the last forty years, than all Europe put together." What Bright actually said was that the United States had offered the world more "inventions"—not more "information," a claim that even those friendly to the North American experiment would have been unlikely to make. But the sentiment counts more than the substance. Against Bright, Arnold cites Ernest Renan: "*The countries which, like the United States, have created a considerable popular instruction without any serious higher instruction, will long have to expiate this fault by their intellectual mediocrity, their vulgarity of manners, their superficial spirit, their lack of general intelligence.*" Arnold found himself having to admit that America *was* attempting something serious in higher education, but he thought it quite the wrong thing: "the university of Mr. Ezra Cornell," founded in 1868, the very year of Renan's comments, is "a really noble monument of his munificence, yet seems to rest on a misconception of what culture truly is, and to be calculated to produce miners, or engineers, or architects, not sweetness and light." [13] On Cornell's seal are words attributed to its founder: "I would found an institution where any person can find instruction in any study"—perhaps an idealized version of what Ezra Cornell, a blunt and down-to-earth businessman, may in fact have said. As Morris Bishop, the university's historian, observes, "possibly Cornell actually said something like: 'I'd like to start a school where anybody can study anything he's a mind to.'" [14] But whatever Cornell's exact words, they would have sounded to Arnold like an unwelcome reprise of the theme played early in the century by the Edinburgh reviewers. And in the debate between McCosh and Eliot, a decade after the second edition of *Culture and Anarchy*, Arnold would have found it easy to choose sides; McCosh's pedagogical trinitarianism matched the Arnoldian vision of culture and of the established church as harmonizing religious difference, while Eliot's elective system would have seemed to exemplify the evils of "doing as one likes." [15]

Above all, the United States lacked an established religion, with a consequent excessive tendency, in Arnold's vocabulary, to *Hebraise*, "to sacrifice all other sides of our being to the religious side." Opposed to Hebraism was Hellenism, with its aim of seeing things "as they really are," but of Hellenism in the United States, Arnold saw little sign: "As we have found that the strongest and most vital part of English Philistinism was the Puritan and Hebraising middle-class, and that its Hebraising keeps it from culture and totality, so it is notorious that the people of the United States issues from this class, and reproduces its tendencies,—its narrow conception of man's spiritual range and of his one thing needful. From Maine to Florida, and back again, all America Hebraises." However disputatious, these words were in some North American quarters waiting to be heard. [16]

Though Arnold must have known that no church was likely

to be established in the United States, much of his program appealed to American instincts: the sponsor of his visits in the 1880s was Andrew Carnegie, for whom Arnold provided, it has been said, "an ethical vocabulary, a spiritual orientation, and an intellectual stance that facilitated [his] self-justification."[17] Perhaps Arnold even consciously directed his gospel of culture and perfectibility, first of all, to his North American audience. Unlike Newman, with his brooding sense of sin, Arnold spoke a language of public optimism that embodied Victorian and transatlantic attitudes alike. Like others who have shared his public convictions, he was capable of darker private utterance—capable in "Dover Beach" of imagining ignorant armies fighting in a world with "neither joy, nor love, nor light / Nor certitude, nor peace, nor help for pain"—but as the apostle of public culture Arnold maintained a relentless optimism about the good that might be done if society were to enter the saving embrace of Hellenism.

Arnold does not renounce "Hebraism," for "the final aim of both Hellenism and Hebraism, as of all great spiritual disciplines, is no doubt the same: man's perfection or salvation." But "culture, and the harmonious perfection of our whole being, and what we call totality," the hallmarks of Arnoldian salvation, appeal to the visionary side of the American character and the nation's sense of itself as marked by special destiny, a city on a hill—a vision shared by Charles Eliot, the Unitarian heir of William Bradford's band of dissenters, however different from Arnold's were the means Eliot thought best suited to the job—while at the same time they appealed to the author of *The Gospel of Wealth* and to custodians of the social order. Not only a way of seeing life whole, culture also is "the most resolute enemy of anarchy," and because "the very framework and exterior order of the State . . . is sacred," the religion of culture and perfection venerates the institutions of the state. In the first edition of *Culture and Anarchy* Arnold included a comment of his father's from an unpublished letter: "As for rioting, the old Roman way

of dealing with *that* is always the right one; flog the rank and
file, and fling the ringleaders from the Tarpeian Rock!" In the
second edition he struck it out, probably realizing that flinging
rioters from the Tarpeian rock, however desirable, might not
seem to square perfectly with his vision of sweetness and light.[18]

In American higher education, the twentieth century has belonged in large part to Arnold's followers, who have grafted
onto Eliot's evolutionary model of the university a contrasting model that sanctifies the idea of a harmonious, secure, and
politically stable culture. At the same time, Newman's Catholic humanism, though not much reflected in curricular wars,
still appeals to skeptics who resist equally the cultural religion
of Arnold, on the one hand, and the scientific religion of the
research university, on the other.

V

'Great Changes Are Impending'

The Politics of Counter-revolution,
1884-1909

As an educational revolutionary who actually succeeded but also understood the normal tidal flows of history, Eliot might almost have guessed that the free elective system would face a counter-revolution. And he lived until 1926, more than long enough to see it take place. Only six years before his death at the age of 86, he wrote a friend, not about the counter-revolution in the curriculum as such, but about what he felt as repudiations of democracy, especially on the part of the Boston aristocracy represented by a generation of Adamses: "I should like to be saved from loss of faith in democracy as I grow old and foolish. I should be very sorry to wind up as the three Adamses did. I shall not, unless I lose my mind."[1] One of the three Adams brothers whose example Eliot intends to avoid will play a part here.

Eliot had succeeded not by fully converting everyone to his beliefs, nor by dogmatism or brutality, but by reflecting aspirations that spurred the creation of American research universities, and by the length and force, personal and political, of his presidency. Eliot's revolution at Harvard was, at Cornell, Andrew Dickson White's revolution; at Stanford, David Starr

Jordan's; at Johns Hopkins, Daniel Coit Gilman's. But Cornell, Stanford, and Hopkins were new creations, whereas Harvard was the nation's oldest university. A "revolution" there, whatever premonitory moments may have come before it (such as Ticknor's reform proposals), was a real revolution, overturning more than two centuries of collegiate practice. At the same time, it quite predictably generated longings for some vanished past, as events at the end of Eliot's tenure and immediately after were to prove.

In 1888 young Barrett Wendell, whom Eliot had brought onto the faculty and who would become one of Harvard's best known professors of literature, wrote in his private journal of Eliot's strength and openness to disagreement, which resulted "often" in his being voted down: "Popular belief has it that Eliot has surrounded himself with a company of followers who do what he tells them to do, with almost religious devotion; in fact, there is a body of men so independent as to be almost unmanageable—fifty or sixty Mugwump parties of one." It was this ability to manage the almost unmanageable and not to resent opposition that made Eliot, in Wendell's account, so formidable a leader. Although he would later disagree deeply with his president, the young Wendell found Eliot irresistible, at least humanly speaking. By 1889, investigations of teaching and discipline under the elective system had already begun, and Wendell commented with concern, "One thing that interests me now is to determine how far the matter is genuine on the part of the malcontents; and how far a half-unconscious organization of a wish to smash Eliot." "Few things," he says, "bother me more now than radically to disagree with the president," for "I am forced to admit that whoever disagrees with him is apt to prove mistaken. Yet nothing could be further from truth than the vulgar notion that he imposes himself on his subordinates, either by brute force—like McCosh, who used to pound the table at Princeton until opposition was silenced—or by a more subtle exercise of his power. He simply reasons—and more convincingly than anyone else I know." Eliot, in Wendell's estimate, was far-seeing, honest, disinterested, and wise.[2]

At the time, Wendell was still an assistant professor in his early thirties, and his awestruck account of Eliot's abilities and "devotion to the college"—"so deep, so earnest, so passionate, that one cannot think of it without a throb of loyalty"—no doubt points up the subtle exercise of power from which Wendell wants to exonerate him.[3] The "new direction" in education, as it was called in the Eliot-McCosh debate, owed so much in the common opinion to Eliot's personal stamina and skill that it was at risk almost from the beginning. Paradoxically, free election might have fared better in the long run if it had not been so deeply associated with one man.

When Eliot retired, rich in years and honors, his curriculum was conspicuously in jeopardy. Some thought it encouraged too much specialization, some that it let students off too easily, others that it failed to deliver the values of the liberal education that Oxford (and Cambridge, too) had refashioned. Since these criticisms were mutually compatible, the forces of resistance were powerfully aligned. Yet Eliot's standing was incomparably high. Symptomatic of the uneasy situation was the mood at the time of his retirement, in June 1909—one of even more ambiguity than usually attaches to moments of institutional transition. The president-designate, A. Lawrence Lowell, a firm opponent of free election, was restrained in praising the retiring president. And to Barrett Wendell, who had increasingly disagreed with "the orthodox doctrine of Eliot—that education is a specialized training for a specific end," fell the assignment of writing a Phi Beta Kappa ode to be presented on July 1, 1909, a doubly difficult task because Wendell was not born a poet and because the occasion demanded that he celebrate Eliot's achievements—as he did, lavishly, in his title, "De Praeside Magnifico."[4] The ode cost him considerable psychic energy and, in the outcome, suffered from a tormented obscurity that embodied the complications of loyalty and dissent induced in Wendell by Eliot's 40 years as president and his rare personal distinction.

Before Wendell read his ode, Woodrow Wilson, then president of Princeton, unfriendly to the elective system, and not a little sensitive to the relative standing of Princeton and Harvard, had delivered the Phi Beta Kappa oration. Wendell later described the occasion to a friend, reporting that Wilson had "pointed out the error of Eliot's ways without mention of him; and greatly commended himself to such as love the prospect of Harvard above the retrospect"—a discreet summary of an address in which Wilson had gone so far as to say that the American college, having "lost its definiteness of aim," had arrived at a state of "all but complete disorganization."[5]

Of his own effort Wendell remarked, "God help me." His struggle "to say what I think about Eliot, in a manner at once true and—to one who does n't look too deep—laudatory," yielded the most tortuous lines of the poem, an example of what the academic mind can (and cannot) do when faced with a desperately uncomfortable task:

> As Edwards, holding Calvin's precepts true,
> Preached them to practice, made them live anew,
> So Eliot now asserts our happier state,
> Edwards of Channing—each securely great.

What this means, Wendell tried to explain to another friend who was English and therefore unfamiliar with the North American scene, is that just as Jonathan Edwards, following Calvin on the assumption of human depravity, managed to get "fatally away from life," so Eliot, following William Ellery Channing's "dogmatic assumption of human perfectibility," did the same: "Just so, I think, Eliot carried to complete absurdity the . . . philosophic dogmas of Channing—that human nature is in itself perfectible. The influence of Edwards is now extinct, except as a matter of history. So, I believe, will that of Eliot . . . be in two or three generations." Probably Wendell was relieved in his faintheartedness to be able to tell his English friend, much puzzled by the lines, "Even here, I think, the full meaning has been hardly remarked." Whether Wendell is correct to attribute Eliot's thought so much to Channing's influence matters less than the convolutions of the ode; they are symptoms of a delicate institutional system suffering acute premonitions of change.[6]

As the limitations of Eliot's system made themselves felt, given especially the American context, in which students come to universities less well grounded in learning and more heterogeneous in social composition than their counterparts in Oxford or Berlin, free election was seen increasingly as having created a political as well as an intellectual empty space. And because it was empty, it cried out to be occupied. Nothing could be more tempting, in a competitive and newly professionalized environment, than open territory. Though it would be another decade before Columbia's required course "Contemporary Civilization" entered the curriculum, jockeying for a position of intellectual primacy became the rule early.

Then as now, the chief claimants for dominance in the cause of liberal education were the disciplines of history, on the one hand, and of literature, as represented largely by departments of English and modern languages, on the other. Even in England, the grip of classical studies had been broken by the end of the century, a volume titled *Essays on a Liberal Education*, edited by F. W. Farrar, then a master at Harrow and later dean of Canterbury, having signaled a change in the intellectual climate as early as 1867; in it the young Henry Sidgwick, later Knightbridge Professor at Cambridge and a distinguished moral philosopher, had challenged the claims of classical training to a monopoly of educational virtue.[7] And in the North American environment classics had never rooted itself so deeply as at Oxford or Cambridge. Nor was philosophy or mathematics in a strong position. If any discipline were to occupy the citadel at the heart of the curriculum, it would have to be history, modern literature, or—as eventually happened—some hybrid of the two. By the same token, if a vision of Arnoldian culture were to be realized in American higher education, it would have to be on terms provided by the blocs of "history" and "literature." No matter how strenuous the efforts to bring in other departments and disciplines—and Columbia's "Contemporary Civilization" was a serious attempt to do so—nothing as yet has decisively altered this power alignment. For one thing, departments of modern literature and history between them make up a very large proportion of the usual university faculty in the humanities. At the ballot box, numbers count.

Yet this understanding of the situation comes with hindsight. At the turn of the century, given the dramatic changes of the previous decades, the situation seemed fluid, hence susceptible to new beginnings. It was this lure that inspired one reformer to make a radical proposal that, had it been put in place, would have bypassed some of the struggles of this century. This was Charles Francis Adams, who in a 1906 Phi Beta Kappa address at Columbia described a scheme to reorganize American higher education, or at least education at Harvard, from the ground up. The interest of the scheme, some of whose features were actually to be adopted, lies in its vivid sense of American university education as still in formation, in its demonstration of the spell that Oxford and Cambridge worked on the American mind, and in its program for achieving a new version of liberal education without surrendering the values of specialization, by then too firmly entrenched ever to be wholly set aside.

A businessman, a historian, a reformer of public schools in Quincy, Massachusetts, a longtime overseer of Harvard College, a grandson of John Quincy Adams, a brother of Henry Adams, an unimpeachable Brahmin—and one of the Adamses whom Eliot in his eighties hoped not to emulate—Charles Francis Adams had a standing in the academy that could scarcely now be replicated. And as a member of Eliot's loyal opposition, he had grown ever more convinced that the elective system was misconceived. In the address that he published as "Some Modern College Tendencies," the bland title masking a fierce attack, though of a politeness that befitted a septuagenarian pillar of the educational establishment, he proposed not patching and papering over but starting afresh.

Adams's recommendations, based on what he regarded as flaws in his own education, were to repudiate free election and to construct a new college system within the university: "In the case of Harvard . . . I would, were it in my power, discontinue absolutely, and wholly break up, the traditional academic system. Harvard College, save in name and continuity, should cease to exist." It is an iconoclasm inspired by 40 years of Eliot's benevolent rule, and such as perhaps could only be voiced by someone who had announced, a paragraph earlier, "A very solid satisfaction exists for me in the consciousness that I am a Harvard man"; and who had gone on to say, tongue not apparently in cheek, "I dare say in Great Britain there are very many excellent educational institutions at Manchester or at Paisley; none the less I should much prefer being an Oxonian or a Cantab. So with us." What his Columbia audience thought of this may lie beyond reach.[8]

The new Harvard, as Adams conceived it, would be a group of independent Oxford-like colleges, each able to set its own tuition, each with its own academic "specialty," each with its own master, and in each of which "the master should know every student"—a more complete version, that is, of the "house" or "college" system that would come to Harvard and Yale by mid-century and an anticipation of The Claremont Colleges, founded in California in the 1920s, or of the University of California's campus at Santa Cruz, dating from the 1960s. Curricular requirements would be tailored by "the immediate advice and impulse of the master . . . acting on personal knowledge of the individual student" and be based on a taxonomy of mental faculties. All this because, Adams says, "I have come to regard the elective system in its present form of development as an educational fad, and a very mischievous one." For a person of his impeccable standing—and a four-term member of Harvard's overseers—to call the elective system a mischievous fad, at a moment far into the fourth decade of Eliot's presidency, was almost to guarantee the truth of what Adams foretold in a supplementary note added to his published text: "One thing only seems undeniable: The present is, in America, a period of academic transition, and great changes are immediately impending." About that, he was perfectly right.[9]

Yet his scheme could only have run afoul of interests newly established in the academy. If the disciplines hoped to seize the opportunity offered by the vacancy at the center of the curriculum, so did Adams, but in a fashion that would have disrupted divisional and departmental structures and their associated patterns of influence. Furthermore, even if the scheme had not threatened disruption, the theory of mental faculties on which it depended had lost much of its explanatory force. Adams's was mostly a quixotic cause, yet in a sense all the more revelatory, making it possible better to understand what did follow by comparison with what did not.

In its tripartite nature, Adams's taxonomy of the faculties reflected habits of thought that also carved out the trinity of the humanities, social sciences, and natural sciences, a trinity that accommodates divisional and departmental interests as Adams's does not. All the faculties, he thought, "group themselves under three distinct heads: first, and highest, the imaginative; second, the reasoning; and third, the observing." Literature and art represent the work of the imaginative faculty; logic and mathematics, that of the reasoning power; and empirical science, that of the observing power. Of the first, Shakespeare is the exemplar; of the second, Newton; and of the third, Darwin. And to be liberally educated is to have "adequately developed" all three faculties.[10]

But, Adams imagines being asked, "where . . . is history and political economy? Where physics, metaphysics, and moral philosophy? The idea of calling a man educated who knows nothing of these branches of knowledge!" He answers as proponents of liberal education have always answered when taxed with having omitted the one or two things needful: namely, by asserting that whatever is included enables the student to undertake whatever has been left out. Liberal education prepares for whatever may come: "To him who can imagine, reason, observe and express himself, all knowledge becomes an open book." And for all the genius that enabled him to "rewrite" Genesis, Darwin's imaginative powers were "naturally defective," so much so that late in life, as Adams recounts with a hint of gratification, he lost all pleasure in poetry, "including Shakespeare." What "Darwin's mind educationally called for, as he himself later noted, was literary development and mathematical training." It is a clever touch, reminiscent in its way of McCosh's resourceful use of Spencer, thus to point out the sense of diminished human experience in the sage whose rewrite of Genesis helped bring the free elective system into being.[11]

The fatal flaws of Adams's scheme show up in any calculation of its institutional results, were it to have been put in effect. Of the fields competing seriously for center stage, literature would have been helped and history severely hurt. Literature represents the imaginative faculty, and imagination is highest of the faculties, while history is no more than first among all the subjects that are unaccounted for, a product of the combined powers of imagination, reason, and observation. One can imagine what (for example) Harvard's most redoubtable historian, Charles Homer Haskins, would have thought of that. Among other fields, logic and mathematics would have gained ground, but what of all those areas lumped together as derivative? The imaginative faculty could be trained by the experience of art and literature, that of reasoning by logic and mathematics, and that of observation by attention to the world of things and of nature. Yet even if this taxonomy had carried more conviction, Adams's plan runs up at every turn against the territorial realities of the divided university. Despite the appearance of open possibilities, too much was already at stake to entertain so radical a revision.

Meanwhile, the disciplinary forces of "history" and of "literature" were gathering about the unoccupied center, and "history" had already established a position of strength appealing to the vision of the United States as a chosen land. In the Iowa legislature of 1884, State Senator Preston M. Sutton had spoken in favor of a more liberal, less exclusively technical curriculum at what was then Iowa State Agricultural College. In his speech, he mounted a defense of historical learning that academic historians, in their hearts, would not be sorry to have heard:

> It has been suggested that History is properly a preparatory study, but it is not. It may be contended that History should be completed before entering college, but it cannot be. The best colleges and universities of the country admit it. There is not a respectable college in the country but makes History one of its leading and most essential studies. . . . History is not only absolutely essential to learning but history may be said to be learning itself. Learning without history is Hamlet with Hamlet left out.

This homespun eloquence soars even higher when Sutton turns from history in general to that of the United States in particular: "There is nothing that America is so proud of as her history. Nothing so inspires the American heart to high ambition as the study of American history, and yet we have a college pretending to give a liberal education with her doors locked against history." At the heart of Sutton's appeal lies America's manifest destiny.[12]

Sutton's speech coincided almost exactly in time with the founding of the American Historical Association, organized at Saratoga, New York, on September 10, 1884, and incorporated by Congress five years later. The annual meetings of the association regularly considered questions of pedagogy. In 1905 and

1906 the members took up the curriculum in higher education, with Haskins, of Harvard, chairing a session in 1905 called "The First Year of College Work in History" and Max Farrand, of Stanford, chairing another in 1906 called "History in the College Curriculum." In each session representatives from different universities and colleges reported on their own institutional practices. These reports are not exhilarating. Historians had come far in a few decades, however, and their success assured them a major role in constructing the modern curriculum.

Haskins's opening remarks in 1905, heavy with portent, embody the sense of these large but not unwelcome responsibilities as well as of great changes impending: "The most difficult question which now confronts the college teacher of history seems, by general agreement, to be the first year of the college course." That is so because the teaching of history "has worked down"—a paradigm for curricular change—"into the sophomore and often into the freshman year." The historians were gladly burdened, that is, by success: "The first college course in history in all our larger institutions attracts a large number of students, in some cases as many as four hundred, so that the management of a large class adds another element to the problem." [13] The real problem was to consolidate these gains. From this effort, as Gilbert Allardyce has observed, would emerge the courses in "Western Civilization" that came for many to represent the very essence of American liberal education. [14]

If historians were strongly placed by 1906 and hoping to improve on their position, the forces of modern literature were less well settled—though the Modern Language Association of America had been founded in 1883 and had engaged in soul-searching about issues named in the titles of two articles, "The College Course in English Literature, How It May Be Improved" and "The Place of English in the College Curriculum," in the first volume of the association's journal (1884–85), then called *Transactions of the Modern Language Association of America* and later, *Publications of the Modern Language Associa-*

tion or *PMLA*.[15] Why did modern literature take hold more slowly than history? In the first place, modern literature still had to compete with classics—the last traces of Harvard's Latin requirement as a condition of entrance did not disappear until the mid-twentieth century—and with the belief that reading literature, especially ancient literature, in translation was no substitute for the real thing. In the second place, while the field of history, though sliced into segments of time and place, was conceptually united, modern literary fields were divided against themselves: on the one hand was literature itself; on the other, dominant at the level of research, was language. While history had a relatively easy time working its way down from graduate teaching and research into the early undergraduate years, graduate work in English and the modern languages meant philology, not something readily transplanted into a course for hundreds of beginners. Literature needed therefore to be split off from philology.

But it also needed, in the third place, a sense of purpose and value equivalent to that which Sutton voiced, in the case of history, before the Iowa legislature. That sense of purpose and value would be achieved by various means, none more conclusive than the benign influence of "the humanities," the conceptual category that gave literature its halo of the sacred. Until the humanities—an old category newly constituted—secured their place in the unfolding trinity of knowledge, literature labored under the disadvantage of sharing accommodations with its awkward bedfellow. "The Place of English in the College Curriculum," in the first volume of transactions of the Modern Language Association, was the work of Theodore W. Hunt, of Princeton. He begins by referring to the trinity that McCosh defended against Eliot in the same year: "It is now customary among the most advanced students of modern education to divide the area of collegiate studies into the three great departments of Science, Philosophy, Language and Literature."[16] Who these "advanced students of modern education" were,

other than McCosh, is uncertain. But in the contest for curricular preeminence, the ungainly pairing of "Language" and
"Literature" stands out. To escape this awkward union, literature needed the good offices of "the humanities." [17]

In 1908, then, appeared a collection of essays with a title that
gathered literature—or "letters," as in Oxford's *literae humaniores*—under the old protective cover of "the humanities": *Literature and the American College: Essays in the Defense of the
Humanities*. This was Irving Babbitt's first book. A teacher of
French at Harvard since 1894, he had seen the free elective
system at first hand and, like Charles Francis Adams, knew
that with Eliot's coming retirement as president, other changes
were bound to follow. *Literature and the American College*, an
early manifesto of what was to be called (over Babbitt's ob-
jections) neo-humanism or "the new humanism," names the
enemy forthrightly: not only Rousseau but, more pressingly,
Charles Eliot, Spencer, and Darwin. Of those on the side of the
humanities, the most prominent name is Arnold's.

As Barrett Wendell would in his Phi Beta Kappa ode the
next year, Babbitt handled Eliot delicately; not to do so would
have been less than magnanimous, and Babbitt's humanism depended on a sort of dogmatic magnanimity. (Allen Tate would
later call it, less charitably, "a kind of moral Fascism.") [18] It was
inevitable, Babbitt says, "in dealing with college education that
I should discuss the role of President Eliot. It was also inevitable, in the case of one who has exercised so many-sided an
influence on his time, that I should fall very short of a rounded
estimate." In this unrounded estimate, Eliot's lineage is that of
Bacon and Rousseau—even though, Babbitt anxiously adds,
"President Eliot's character and personal distinction, we need
scarcely say, do not connect him with either Bacon or Rousseau." Character and personal distinction aside, Eliot is also a
Spencerian because Spencer, too, is a descendant of Babbitt's
Rousseau. And, if Eliot is a Spencerian, he is a Darwinian as
well. Again like Charles Francis Adams, Babbitt takes Darwin,

the scientist of impaired literary sensibilities, as a cautionary example: "Every one remembers the passage in which Darwin confesses with much frankness that his human appreciation of art and poetry had been impaired by a one-sided devotion to science." [19]

But Babbitt has no doubt that the free elective system—"educational *laissez faire* such as prevailed at Harvard in the eighties and nineties"—"is plainly doomed," and it is this familiar sense of the old order's passing, of a space therefore waiting to be filled, that gave neo-humanism its peculiar energy. And behind it all lie the schoolmasterly affirmations of Arnold: "The aim, as Matthew Arnold has said in the most admirable of his critical phrases, is to see life steadily and see it whole." [20]

By 1908, Babbitt could already see changes that promised a better future. In particular, Harvard had established in 1903 a program of "Honors in Literature," with roots in Oxford's honors programs. It encouraged independent reading, tested "the student's powers of assimilation," and most important, subordinated research and philology to literature and appreciation. Unlike other honors programs that would follow, it required not "even so much research as is represented by a thesis." And it combined the study of classical and modern literatures, requiring the knowledge of one ancient language and one modern language besides English, thus fulfilling practical imperatives in a nation where classics had not dominated the curriculum. Perceptive in his conviction that "the ancient humanities" could not (even in Oxford and certainly not in the United States) maintain a "haughty isolation," Babbitt saw the new program as combining forces that would march together under the banner of the humanities and, he fondly wished, put to rest the "unprofitable antagonism between ancients and moderns." [21]

In such an entente lay the hope not only of undoing what Eliot had done but of setting matters right even on the farthest edge of the continent, where, in a university recently founded, a student might enter with no Latin or Greek, no other languages, and no non-scientific subject other than English composition—and thereafter graduate "on completing a certain number of hours' work in mechanical engineering." If Stanford's model were to prevail, Babbitt feared, the Bachelor of Arts degree might "soon come to be granted to a student as a reward for getting his professional training as a plumber!" The exclamation point is Babbitt's own.[22]

The strength of neo-humanism, the oppositional tensions within the camp of literature, and the wistfulness of Babbitt's hope for a truce between ancients and moderns can all be measured by looking ahead to another battle of the books two decades later. Early in 1930 Babbitt's disciple Norman Foerster edited a collection of essays by (among others) T. S. Eliot, Babbitt, and Paul Elmer More, another founding member of the movement; its none-too-modest title was *Humanism and America: Essays on the Outlook of Modern Civilisation*. Then in the same year appeared a counter-manifesto, *The Critique of Humanism: A Symposium*, edited by C. Hartley Grattan. Of its contributors, none was yet 40 years old, and they included almost all the young insurgents of American letters: R. P. Blackmur, Kenneth Burke, Malcolm Cowley, Lewis Mumford, Allen Tate, Edmund Wilson, Yvor Winters, and others. The results are often quotable, and a few examples will illustrate how much had changed in the space of two decades. No longer was the intellectual and institutional standing of the humanities in question, a point that had been decisively made, but rather their substance. These critics of neo-humanism stand in the same relationship to Babbitt and his colleagues as did William Hamilton, in the mid-nineteenth century, to Edward Copleston and his fellow Oxonians. What the critics of Babbitt's agenda, moderns all, looked for was a tougher-minded, more realistic, more socially responsible humanism than that of their predecessors. Yet had they been able to see their situation in the perspective of time, they could have agreed with the moderns of the seventeenth century, that they stood higher than the ancients because they stood upon their shoulders.

The neo-humanists, their critics said, offer warmed-over Arnold: "There is probably little in their philosophy that could not be extracted, and in a richer form, from Matthew Arnold." They ignore social realities: "What . . . has Humanism to do with the scene outside my window: with the jobless men who saunter in the dusk, or the dying village, or the paper mill abandoned across the river?" They do not understand contemporary literature and art or recognize its humanizing virtues: "I never *saw* a telephone till I saw it in one of Charles Sheeler's drawings." And they represent, in all, an arid, outworn, antipopulist humanism, derivative and ill-matched to American needs.[23]

In misreading *Antigone*, says Edmund Wilson, Babbitt has "almost succeeded in giving Sophocles and Plato the aspect of pious English dons." In fact he "has turned Sophocles into something worse and even more alien to his true nature: he has turned him into a Harvard Humanist."[24] To the tough, young Edmund Wilson, nothing could be more debilitating than the gentility of Oxford and Harvard, of Arnold and Babbitt. Yet the array of talent here lined up against the genteel tradition shows how far "humanism" and "the humanities" had come. Babbitt, More, and their colleagues had opened doors to a new curriculum. Yvor Winters, as perceptive as he was sometimes curmudgeonly, knew this: "One's objection to the Humanists is not to their humanism but to their lack of it."[25] The forces of "literature," like those of "history," had gone on the march, rejecting as a forced and inexpedient marriage the previously solid union between philology and literature. The "modern" successors of the "ancient" neo-humanists were gainers by it.

Literary neo-humanism had support in high places, too. In 1902 the presidency of Princeton fell to Woodrow Wilson, who in 1896 had published *"Mere Literature" and Other Essays*, reissued in 1897 and again in 1900; the message of the title essay, originally published in 1893, was that "mere literature will keep us pure and keep us strong."[26] Furthermore, 1909 and 1910 saw the publication of *The Harvard Classics*, Charles Eliot's editorial effort to make good his claim that "a five-foot shelf would hold books enough to give in the course of years a good substitute for a liberal education in youth to any one who would read them with devotion, even if he could spare but fifteen minutes a day." In the last of the 50 volumes, the materials are indexed into categories of, first, "subject-matter" and, second, "literary form." Under the second category, the final subheading is "Narrative Poetry and Prose Fiction," a class of "mere literature," including Homer, Virgil, and Dante, that made Eliot, child of the Puritans that he was, a little uneasy: "In this section we have the largest proportion of what frankly professes to be the literature of entertainment." Even so, he manages an expression of literature's importance that Babbitt and Woodrow Wilson could have smiled on: "No less than the most weighty philosophy or the most informing history or science, then, do these stories in prose and poetry deserve their place among the essential instruments of mental and moral culture."[27] Yet Eliot is happiest, no doubt, with "subject-matter." The very first subheading under "subject-matter" is "The History of Civilization." In its conceptual framework (as thus laid out by Eliot and his "assistant," William Allan Neilson, of Harvard's English Department) *The Harvard Classics* anticipates a future in which "mere literature" and "the history of civilization," understood as Western civilization, would more or less equally define the arena of liberal education, newly re-established when the doctrine of free election was overturned.[28]

VI

Between the Wars

Aspirations to Order

The aim of the course is to inform the student of the more outstanding and influential factors in his physical and social environment. The chief features of the intellectual, economic, and political life of to-day are treated and considered in their dependence on and difference from the past. The great events of the last century in the history of the countries now more closely linked in international relations are reviewed, and the insistent problems, internal and international, which they are now facing are given detailed consideration.

Announcement of "Contemporary Civilization,"
Columbia, 1919–20

Generally speaking, all freshmen are either now or soon to be voters. Does not the University owe them a duty as such? If our tritest sayings are true these freshmen are destined to become leaders in their respective communities. They are forming the political, economic, and social ideas that will characterize that leadership. And they are forming them now while the air is full of strange doctrines and without waiting for a critical and scholarly insight. Can the University not render a substantial social service by providing a sound basis of elementary scientific facts and principles by which the validity of these doctrines may be tested?

"Reorganization of Undergraduate Instruction,"
Stanford, 1920

When they discussed the first-year course in history, the members of the American Historical Association labored under an empirical difficulty in 1905. What was history in the first year to be the history *of*? In practice, there was agreement that it should be the history of Western Europe. But of what period? Harvard's answer was the fourth to the fourteenth century; Wisconsin's, 395 to 1500; Yale's, from the fall of Rome to 1870. At Minnesota, students with one year of high school preparation took European history, 31 B.C.E. to 1500 C.E.; those with two years of preparation took English constitutional history to the seventeenth century. And at Vassar, historical method came first: "An intelligent understanding of the tools of historical study and a knowledge of how to use them would seem to be essential to the young student even if such knowledge is gained at a sacrifice of some of the details of the Hundred Years' war, the war of the Roses, the struggles of Francis I and Charles V, or even of the interminable struggles between the various Ottos and the contemporary Popes." Of the historians who reported on their curricula, only Lucy M. Salmon, of Vassar, and "her colleague, Miss Ellery," who stood in for her at the meeting, seem able (with Edward Gibbon) to have regarded history in certain of its aspects as a record of interminable struggles between various Ottos and various Popes.[1] No others seem to have shared this (many would think) enlightened view. But all could appreciate the reason behind the session: the hope of discovering new common ground.

The timely intervention of the First World War is usually thought to have inspired a more general consensus, but this interpretation, accurate so far as it goes, cloaks a more tangled web of cause and effect. Certainly the war, as John Higham has pointed out, brought new attention to the immigrant population in America along with "more widespread concern than Americans had ever before felt over the immigrants' attachment to their adopted country" and, therefore, more widespread concern for the homogeneities of citizenship.[2] And, it is also true, Columbia's "Contemporary Civilization" arose from the ashes of the university's course "War Aims." But aspirations to consensus had been gathering; whether they might have been realized, to the extent they were, without the catalyst of war and the boost it gave to xenophobia is uncertain: it is at least possible.[3] At the same time, war or no war, the academic consensus was never to become complete, in part because principles are one thing, personalities and private domains another. Harvard's introductory course in history belonged to Charles Homer Haskins from 1904 to 1925, and Harvard was one university that did not follow Columbia in creating a "Western Civilization" requirement, although some concerns elsewhere associated with the requirement found their way into Harvard's freshman English curriculum. The supposed universality of "Western Civilization" is an artifact comprising nostalgia, desire, and the sustaining belief in an assimilationist mythology. But that is not to say that nothing significant happened.

Although the arrival of "Western Civilization" effectively capped the pedagogical campaign that occupied Haskins and his fellow delegates in 1905, historians at first could have felt disenfranchised. When Columbia's new course, a collaboration between economics, government, philosophy, and history, was established in 1919, existing requirements in both philosophy and history were dropped, and one of Columbia's faculty would later report, with dramatic prematurity, the death of parochial interests: "It meant a decisive renunciation of departmental parochialism and an abandonment once and for all of the provincial interests that divided and can still divide the academic community."[4] And at Stanford the new requirement was called "Problems of Citizenship," as it was also at Dartmouth, and took "political, economic, and social science" for its basis. History was not banished, but as one requirement among others, it was not squarely at the heart of the curriculum. Or not, at least, in theory—or for the time being.

But whatever historians temporarily gave up, events proved

them in time the natural custodians of the requirement. For the 1905 convention, Dana C. Munro, of Wisconsin, though unable to attend, submitted a statement ascribing Wisconsin's choice of medieval history for the first year to its usefulness in training students for the responsibilities of citizenship: "For the great mass of students the purpose of such a course . . . must be preparation for a broad, enlightened citizenship. They must have brought before them a point of view from which they can understand the civilization of their own times. Moreover, they must be led to form historical judgments. Mediaeval history seems the field which best serves these two purposes." Since he was co-editor of *Mediaeval Civilization* (1904), a collection of excerpts from European historians that he and his colleague George C. Sellery assigned in the course, Munro's objectivity might not stand up to careful scrutiny. But medieval history, conceived as the springboard to enlightened citizenship, enabled him to claim impartiality: "It is, especially in the earlier portion, remote enough from the burning questions of our own day so that students may be led to take unbiased positions on the subjects which agitated the men of that time. They can grasp the fact that every important question of public policy has two sides, which can be held honestly by men of equal ability."[5]

Medieval history, that is, offers some of the same mental and ideological exercise as formal debate—and some of the same safety. But when the war ended America's isolation from the burning questions of international policy, something nearer the bone was needed or, perhaps, became *acceptable*. Thus Columbia created its "Contemporary Civilization," "C.C." as it came to be called, probably the most famous course ever in the American curriculum; Stanford and Dartmouth created their "Problems of Citizenship"; and at Stanford "Problems of Citizenship" became after little more than a decade "Western Civilization." From such contingencies the legend was waiting to be made.

The titular quaintness (to our ears) of "Problems of Citizenship" indicates a source, other than and at the outset at least as vital as the hunger of historians, behind the tradition that was soon to be: namely, the American institutions of "Civics" and education in citizenship. Not only were Stanford's and Dartmouth's courses called "Problems of Citizenship," but the University of Missouri called its requirement "Problems of American Citizenship, Including English Composition," and Williams College offered "American National Problems," all these courses thus perpetuating the immigration-inspired movement toward education in citizenship that had first come into vogue at the same time as Eliot's elective system was near its zenith. Harvard, then "bursting with the activity of Teutonist historians," was near the forefront of this development, too. Albert Bushnell Hart's "History 13," a survey of U.S. history from 1789 to 1860, was what Barbara Miller Solomon calls a voluntary "must" in the curriculum; and Hart was one of those "Teutonists" who enforced ideas of "Anglo-Saxon superiority" and who prepared the way (for example) for the founding of the Immigration Restriction League early in the twentieth century.[6] Also in the late 1880s and early in 1890, articles appeared in the periodical *Education*, founded in 1880 as *Education: An International Magazine*, that described "preparation for citizenship" at Harvard, Amherst, Smith, Williams, and the schools of Michigan; it was Hart who described Harvard's offerings.[7] And in the 1880s, there arose as well the almost messianic new vocation called "Civics" that would in time produce countless high-school courses and no little adolescent pain.

A history of "Civics" would begin with the unfamiliar and elusive figure of Henry Randall Waite, pastor of the American church in Rome from 1871 to 1874; organizer of a National Reform League, in 1876, that proposed "efforts for the overthrow of every influence, whether represented by parties or individuals, which has a tendency to foster or promote corruption"; and the first to have used the term "civics" to refer to "those branches of science that pertain to the elevation of citizenship." [8] In the mid 1880s, after an influx of immigrants and an industrial downturn had intensified worries about immigration, Waite—himself liberal-minded—founded the American Institute of Civics to promote "with patriotic insistency . . . that special training of all citizens which shall qualify them for the highest service of country." [9] Then in 1894 he became co-editor of the recently founded *American Journal of Politics*, renaming it *The American Magazine of Civics: A Journal of Practical Patriotism* and outfitting it with a smart new red, white, and blue cover. Thus rechristened and spruced up, the magazine lasted only a few years before being absorbed by another periodical, *The Arena*, but the impulse behind its existence would far outlive it.

During its brief run *The American Magazine of Civics* offered a section called "The Civic Outlook," with *"notes and comments concerning affairs of interest to intelligent and patriotic citizens,"* who were invited to send in communications; the "Good Citizenship Activities" section included items from all over; and the doings of the institute's National Lecture Corps were reported, a note announcing in 1897, "Woodrow Wilson, Ph.D., A. I. C. Lecture Corps, has recently delivered his admirable lecture on 'Leaders of Political Thought' in the University Extension courses at Tarrytown, N. Y., and Lancaster, Pa." Articles sometimes addressed economic or historical matters; or, in the case of an article by the Reverend W. G. Puddefoot, the most pressing social issue of the day, "Is the Foreigner a Menace to the Nation?" (Puddefoot thought not). Sometimes they were more purely inspirational, like "Patriotism," by Wilmot H. Goodale, professor of philosophy and civics at Louisiana State University. Patriotism, said Goodale, warming to his peroration, "must be enshrined in the heart of the American citizen with the earliest lessons of his life. He should be indoctrinated in the laws and customs of the land and taught to honor its flag and sing its national songs. Into his mind should be instilled all those principles of courage, fortitude, and patriotism which ever meet in man's loftiest ideals of man." And Goodale closed with a salute to "the grandest country beneath the sun," its citizens singing, "with all the fervor of exalted patriotism"—"My country, 'tis of thee. . . ." Lest this Goodalian rhetoric give an unbalanced idea of the magazine's content, however, it should be added that the same issue included Eugene V. Debs's fervent defense, "The Cry of 'Anarchist.'"[10]

In Waite's scheme, "Civics" as a "science" incorporated, first, "Ethics," defined by E. Benjamin Andrews, president of Brown University and a member of Waite's institute, as "The Doctrine of Duties in Society"; and then "Civil Polity"; "Law"; "Economics"; and "History." That the universities bore some responsibility for imparting this new science to students can be inferred not only from Woodrow Wilson's and Benjamin Andrews's association with Waite's institute but from Robert Treat Paine's "The Problems of Charity," an address to the National Conference of Charities and Correction that Waite published in 1896. A philanthropist and Harvard graduate (and later a member of the Immigration Restriction League), Paine ended by addressing the universities: "Not in jealousy, but in noble emulation, Yale and Harvard and Columbia, and all the rest, must send their men into the contest for the leadership of the world, not merely with broad and solid foundation of knowledge, not merely with thorough special training in sociologic problems, but, more than all else, with a fiery enthusiasm of human sympathy." The "fiery enthusiasm of human sympathy" is less in tune with the conventions of academic discourse than a "thorough special training in sociologic problems," but the civic benevolism of the courses that blossomed after the war has an unmistakable affinity with citizenship education in the 1880s and with Henry Randall Waite's missionary creation.[11]

Consider some textbooks for the high-school trade produced in the first two decades of the century—for example, *Preparing for Citizenship: An Elementary Textbook in Civics* (1913), dedicated by its author, William Backus Guitteau, to "the teachers in our schools on whom chiefly devolves the great privilege of preparing for citizenship the youth of our land"; or *Advanced Civics: The Spirit, the Form, and the Functions of the American Government* (1905), by the prolific Samuel Eagle Forman—who appears on the title page as S. E. Forman, Ph.D. This textbook appeared in eleven editions between 1905 and 1927, the largest number of them before 1916, and Forman's publications in civics and American history, in their many printings, span four and a half pages of the *National Union Catalogue* of books. It was a boom time for "the great"—and no doubt lucrative—"privilege of preparing for citizenship" the youth of the land.

In Guitteau's text, an ode by Margaret E. Sangster (author of, inter alia, *Winsome Womanhood*) precedes the first chapter. The temptation to quote all of "Casting the First Vote" is great, but that would be harder to justify than in the case of Newman's prose. Taxing though it is to choose from her vision of voting armies, Sangster's second stanza is particularly alluring:

> Clear-eyed, strong-limbed, and sturdy,
>   These honest sons of toil—
> They hold the ballot like a prayer,
> Uplifted through the fateful air,
>   That none our land may spoil.
> In their young manhood everywhere
>   They rise to guard the soil.[12]

That "Civics" was created at roughly the same time as the free elective system speaks to the checks and balances at work in American life. And when Stanford set about to "reorganize undergraduate instruction" after the war, the committee charged with the task spoke in a voice that, if more tempered, closely resembled the civic utterance of Henry Randall Waite: "Generally speaking, all freshmen are either now or soon to be voters. Does not the University owe them a duty as such?"[13]

Yet because the university's public service function does not

square precisely with its critical function or with its felt obligation to provide "liberal" training, there arose from this development tensions that have come to afflict not only education
itself but discourse about its role even more deeply. Courses
on citizenship, for which courses on civilization came to be
surrogates, were bound to take the society of their own origin as a reference point, hence the inward-lookingness and
self-interestedness, from the beginning, of the new tradition.
Hence, too, the strangeness that arises as courses on civilization, and especially courses on Western civilization, are linked
with the liberal ideal. In its canonical version, liberal education
aspires to disinterest, however much it valorizes the experience
of Greece and Rome. From exercises in (say) Latin composition, few would claim that civic awareness as such was apt to
spring, however useful the discipline might be as preparation
for civic responsibilities. As for the history courses that pre-
ceded "Western Civilization," these too could often assert objectivity: medieval history in Dana Munro's account illustrates
how principles held reasonably and honorably may nonetheless differ. Courses in "Western Civilization" could not manage
quite the same appearance of disinterest. This problem Columbia and Stanford handled with different degrees of skill.

In announcing "Contemporary Civilization," Columbia displayed considerable deftness in combining the agendas of liberal and civic education—in particular, through the good
offices of "history." The social agenda can be inferred but does
not obtrude. As the course's first syllabus put it, "We are living
in a world in which there are great and perplexing issues on
which keen differences of opinion have arisen; and it is important now, not less than during the war, that men should understand the forces which are at work in the society of their own
day."[14] This understanding is defined as depending on knowledge of how the present follows and differs from the past—
that is, on a teleological reading of the past as culminating in
the present. On such a reading the tradition of courses on citi-

zenship and civilization rests, and this understanding ensured that historians, however seemingly disenfranchised, would in fact dominate the tradition. Of the texts used in, and in this case created for, "C.C.," the most influential was John Herman Randall's *The Making of the Modern Mind* (1926). Himself a philosopher, Randall had a historical turn of mind, and "history," he announced as he began, is "a human achievement." The teleological bias of his title underlies his account of "the civilization that is our own heritage."[15] In the historical context, metaphors of lineage and inheritance supplant civic "problems." Columbia's strategy in launching "C.C." was not only clever but in the long run determinative.

Stanford's strategy was less adroit, more transparent. The committee that reported to President Ray Lyman Wilbur in 1920 and recommended "Problems of Citizenship" let slip the comment "The air is full of strange doctrines," thus pointing to an opportunity for counter-indoctrination.[16] Probably the makeup of the committee, which was unusual, contributed to this mis-step. It was chaired by Arthur Martin Cathcart, who taught constitutional law and addressed the Commonwealth Club of California in talks such as "What Is Happening to the Constitution?" (1933), in which he questioned the constitutionality of the National Recovery Act; and "Constitutional Freedom of Speech and of the Press" (1935), in which he stressed limitations on free speech. Others of the committee's members came from the English, Chemistry, and Mechanical Engineering departments; and still another, like Cathcart, from the Law School. None came from History. Such a committee, if not necessarily on the lookout for "strange doctrines," might understandably take "citizenship," defined as a matter of "political, economic, and social ideas," more deeply to heart than "history." But when "Problems of Citizenship" first surfaced in the university's course listings for 1923–24, Edgar Eugene Robinson, then 35 years old and a full professor of American history since 1918, was its director, a position he held for the twelve years that the course lasted. In the listing nothing is said of "strange doctrines," but the course's six headings reproduce the style and substance of "Civics." They range from "Bases of Civilization" to "Political Equipment of the Citizen" to "Education for Citizenship," the latter including "such subdivisions as Agencies for Publicity, the Development of Community Life," and, not least, "Opportunities of an Individual in a Democracy." Whereas Columbia's "C.C." had from the start an air of urban *savoir faire*, Stanford's "Problems of Citizenship" had a sort of schoolroom graininess that would need to be polished up.

That is exactly what happened. Between 1923 and 1935, "Problems of Citizenship" grew more sophisticated in content and method, gradually leaving the mannerisms of "Civics" behind—a process that can be discerned in Robinson's introductory lecture in the fall of 1928, "Citizenship in a Democratic World," which survives in printed form (evidently for general distribution) and is included as an appendix here. But in growing more sophisticated, the course brought on its own demise. "Citizenship" having had its day as a high-profile university subject, something new was needed, and in this changed context the faculty voted in 1935 to replace "Problems of Citizenship" with "Introduction to Social Problems" (grouped as a requirement with other options in economics, philosophy, political science, psychology, and sociology) and to substitute "The History of Western Civilization" as the requirement for all. "Introduction to Social Problems" became, in 1946–47, "Introduction to Social Service" and before expiring in 1950–51 shared its place in the course listings with such offerings as "Marriage and the Family." "Citizenship," that is, became a diminishing asset in the university, while "The History of Western Civilization" prospered—and carried with it, as events of more than 50 years would prove, the burden of its civic past. By whatever name, in fact, courses in Western civilization carry symbolic and social obligations almost beyond their capacity to bear. Wise though it was to subsume civics to history and to civilization, and much as it enhanced the standing of the historians, "Western Civilization" has had to perform a balancing act that combines a sense of social stability and centrality with the inquiring objectivity of liberal education, no easy task.

> Lucretius stood in awe before the universe, but he stood aloof; Shelley and Emerson, modern of the moderns, beheld man entering into control of a vaster universe than the Roman poet merely contemplated. When literature expresses the miracle of that control, our common life will be transfigured in wonder, our dreams will lie, not in the impossible, but in the path of our happy destiny, and the gods will walk with us.
>
> John Erskine, "Magic and Wonder
> in Literature," 1916

While historians were consolidating their gains, the professionals of literature stayed on the move, though in more diffuse fashion. Despite the strength of the neo-humanists, their anti-Romantic moral rigor was never incorporated into the required curriculum, although it was and continued until recently to be a powerful presence in individual programs and courses. More conclusive in shaping the curriculum was the tradition, newly labeled if not invented in the late nineteenth and early twentieth century, of "great books," a tradition derived from a combination of Victorian aestheticism and pedagogical impulses, and one that appears (deceptively) as more ideologically neutral than that of the neo-humanists. Under the spell of George Edward Woodberry and his student John Erskine, Columbia played a leading role here, if not so decisively as in the case of "Western Civilization," introducing in 1920 an honors course on great books that became, in 1932, the "Colloquium on Important Books" and then in 1937 developed into "Humanities A," required of all students.[17] While in Cambridge

Irving Babbitt offered antidotes to Romanticism, on Morningside Heights there grew up the more aestheticized cult of "great
books" and the tradition that Robert Hutchins would later alter
for his own revisionary purposes at the University of Chicago.
Distinguishing between expressions of neo-humanism and the
aesthetic of "great books" is easy at the extremes, not always so
easy when these separate tributaries flow together. On the one
hand, no one would mistake John Erskine's vision of Emerson and Shelley as precursors to a new coming of the gods
who "will walk with us" for anything ever imagined by Babbitt, who thought Shelley "the most purely Rousseauistic of
the English romantic poets."[18] On the other hand, Eliot's five-
foot shelf could as well be assigned to either tradition. Both
traditions take inspiration from Arnold yet are at heart quite
distinct.

Other than Arnold, what were the sources of the aesthetic of
"great books"? That is a large question, and a full-scale answer
would have to take into account the imprint on educational
thought of figures as various and as early as Wordsworth and
John Stuart Mill. Their influence (and that of others) helped
direct attention to modern literary texts and produced in turn
the liberalization of liberal education later in the century. In
1898, Dean F. W. Farrar, whose edited collection *Essays on a Liberal Education* some 30 years earlier had challenged the rigorous
classicism of Oxford and Cambridge, published a collection
of his own pieces, originally written for *The Sunday Magazine* of
London (subtitled "For Family Reading"); and this volume he
called *Great Books*. In it he provided a primer in spiritual and aesthetic education for young readers. Indeed "great books," the
works of Shakespeare, Dante, and Milton, offer something like
the aesthetic equivalent of civics: all the essays in Farrar's collection were "*written with the single desire to be of use, especially to
young readers, who in these days, when books are so abnormally multiplied, are apt to overlook the rich treasuries of the immortal teachers
of the past.*" Some of Farrar's inspiration comes from Ruskin:

"All books, as Mr. Ruskin says, may be classed as 'books for the hour or books for all time.'" And some of his motivations, like Ruskin's, come from a sense of their world not only as one in which books are "abnormally multiplied" but as one that quite overflows with print—a habit of mind coeval in its origins with print itself. Though newspapers may be "necessary," "yet the amount of time deplorably wasted by numberless readers in idly devouring scraps of disconnected and vapid intelligence is quite inconceivable." Great books are curative, a way of coping with the dreadful proliferation of the printed word. They are also, of course, "great": "Literature unfolds to us the deepest thoughts which can fill the great heart of humanity. We may, if we choose, find a purer and more exquisite delight in wise reading than in almost anything else." This high Victorian piety remains a hallmark of the "great books" tradition in the hands of Woodberry and Erskine.[19]

Born in 1855, George Edward Woodberry graduated from Harvard early in Eliot's presidency, taught at the University of Nebraska, and served as an editor of *The Nation* before coming to Columbia as professor of comparative literature in 1891. For Woodberry, his student Erskine would say, "literature was life itself,"[20] and this sense of a spiritual art indistinguishable from a spiritual life underlies Woodberry's celebration of Cervantes, Scott, Milton, Virgil, Montaigne, and Shakespeare in *Great Writers* (1907). It is the identity between literature and life, whether as a biographical or a rhetorical construct, that the New Criticism would rise up to challenge. Shakespeare the man, New Criticism would insist, was not the same as "Shakespeare" the author of the sonnets; but for Woodberry, Shakespeare and life, or the life force, were one. The tradition of "great books," as distinct from "the classics," placed a heavy weight on the Bard, a weight that none other than Charles Eliot, ever the modern, effectively foresaw in his 1876 address, "What Is a Liberal Education?": "Greek literature compares with English as Homer compares with Shakspere, that is, as infantile with adult civilization."[21] Bardolatry replaces classicism, and Woodberry worships at the new altar: "The secret of life solves the riddle of Shakspere, whose greatness has no other mystery than the mystery of the greatness of life. He is the spirit of life made manifest in its own dramatic motion, imprisoned, embodied and unveiled in art."[22] Great books capture great life.

Woodberry's *Great Writers* was reprinted in 1912, and in 1928 Erskine published *The Delight of Great Books*, a collection of essays on Chaucer, Malory, Spenser, Shakespeare, and Milton, which was twice reprinted, in 1935 and 1941. The introductory essay, "On Reading Great Books," recommended a Ruskinian test of greatness, repeated re-reading: "Until we have discovered that certain books grow with our maturing experience and other books do not, we have not learned how to distinguish a great book from a book."[23] The "great books" tradition reached its height between the wars, and neither those who deplore nor those who embrace the tradition have much explored the underpinnings of this curious faith.

The evidence, however, leads to the conclusion that, far from being ideologically neutral, the cult of "great books," as certain of its critics have realized or believed, was touched by obsessional concerns about "race," arising from the "nativist" tradition, that flourished in the early decades of the century. These concerns make a large subject, one that has been studied by Thomas F. Gossett in *Race: The History of an Idea in America* (1963), and here is not the place to rehearse the story. Yet two strains of racist thought may be distinguished: on the one hand, a sort of high-minded mystical version, the racism not only of the Comte de Gobineau or of Richard Wagner but also of the Anglo-Saxonist Brahmin Barrett Wendell; on the other hand, the crude redneck version represented by (to choose an egregious example) the likes of Henry F. Suksdorf, whose *Our Race Problems* appeared in 1911. The usefulness of Suksdorf as an example is that of illustrative contrast, the vulgarity of his racism far exceeding anything to be discovered in the "great books" tradition yet suggesting how that more respectable and genteel enterprise shared in the climate of its times.

A more virulent racist than Suksdorf could hardly be invented or imagined, and his book is loaded with assertions that (for instance) "divers countries of fossilized Asia are also beginning to send their heavy and swelling contingents"; that if this "undesirable human element" is "absorbed and assimilated, American manhood and womanhood, and American civilization, will certainly deteriorate"; and that when African-Americans have been persuaded to emigrate voluntarily and "our gates have been closed against further immigration of stagnant, decadent, unprogressive and undesirable ethnic elements from Asia and from eastern and southeastern Europe[,] a new era of unexampled progress will dawn upon the United States. Teutons and Celts will rush to the sunny South, and take the place of the departed Negro. Labor will be ennobled again." And so on, far beyond the limits of endurance.[24]

George Edward Woodberry was not Henry F. Suksdorf. Yet Woodberry shared, ever so politely, in the endemic racism and xenophobia of the early century, and his understanding of literature and "great books" assumes the primacy of what he calls, unhappily to our ears, "the race-mind." No more than the simultaneity of life and literature is "the race-mind" easily understood, but this mythology of race is the subject of lectures Woodberry delivered at the Lowell Institute in Boston in 1903 and published as *The Torch: Eight Lectures on Race Power in Literature* (1905). The first lecture, "Man and the Race," makes especially uncomfortable reading, notwithstanding Woodberry's effort at evolutionary broad-mindedness: "If the aristocracy of the whole white race is so to melt in a world of the coloured races of the earth, I for one should only rejoice in such a divine triumph of the sacrificial idea in history; for it would mean the humanization of mankind." In 1903, however, there is no question where the race-mind expresses itself most profoundly, namely, in Europe, for there Arnold's "best" is best realized: "The literature of Europe is the expression of . . . common genius—the best that man has dreamed or thought or done, has found or been, in Europe—now more brilliant in one capital, now in another as the life ebbs from state to state, and is renewed; for, though it fail here or there, it never ceases. This is the burning of the race-mind, now bright along the Seine, the Rhine and the Thames, as once by the Ganges and the Tiber." And the "race-mind" in Europe burns brightest in the "great books" of its great writers—Spenser, Milton, Wordsworth, and Shelley are Woodberry's examples in *The Torch*— "whose essential greatness and value are due to the degree in which they availed themselves of the race-store."[25]

If Woodberry's racism was not malignantly intended, however twisted his categories, the same is not true of a bizarre outburst by Erskine, so odd as to inspire the question whether it might not, just possibly, be a satire. But apparently not: *The Influence of Women and Its Cure* (1936) is a startling display of habits of mind that opponents have intuited in the "great books" agenda. Fairness requires saying that it is somewhat less distressing than its title or its dedication—"To the Men of America (Those Who Remain)." Though laced with misogynist propositions such as "the woman who will admit she has got what she wanted, exists only in books," *The Influence of Women and Its Cure* is directed at the idleness of women of leisure and (for example) at "the censorship which women exercise upon literature," while at the same time it contains what, in 1936, would have seemed some "advanced" ideas: "Why shouldn't society insist that every woman stick to her maiden name," and "as for the children, why shouldn't they take the name of whichever parent they prefer?"[26] Fairness also requires saying that Erskine has no direct concern here with "great books." By 1936 he had taken leave from Columbia to follow his interests in creative writing and music, and from 1928 to 1937 he served as president of the Juilliard School of Music. If the "great books" are implicated in *The Influence of Women and Its Cure*, it is by association. Yet *The Delight of Great Books* also displayed a dismissive hostility to women who disliked Milton's Eve: "The distinctions [Milton] makes between masculine and feminine psychology have raised the ladies, here and there, to protest." And Erskine's treatment of Eve, despite the evident self-assurance of his own male gallantry, defies charitable interpretation. Of Eve's offering the apple to Adam, Erskine says: "Of course she lies about it when she offers him the apple. I leave it to a misogynist to say that her policy was feminine."[27] Even on the most benign interpretation, the friends of "great books" have some things to answer for. Woodberry and Erskine held beliefs that no longer approach the threshold of acceptability.

When the "great books" finally made their way into the Columbia curriculum as a required course, it was under the rubric of the humanities. When they made their way into the curriculum at Chicago, with the relentless prodding of Robert M. Hutchins, guided by Erskine's student Mortimer Adler, it was as instruments of Hutchins's utopian desire to redesign the university and to redeem "the higher learning in America" from "the confusion that besets it." As president and then as chancellor of the university from 1929, when he was 30, to 1951, Hutchins's hope was to "revitalize metaphysics and restore it to its place in higher learning" and thereby (no modest aim) "be able to establish rational order in the modern world as well as in the universities," a program that would have been congenial to William Hamilton a century earlier in some if not all its aspects.[28] These sentiments are from *The Higher Learning in America* (1936), published in the middle of Hutchins's presidency. In the 1950s, when he was editor-in-chief of *Great Books of the Western World*, his thinking (not surprisingly) shifted in the direction of more capacious "liberal education," designed to ensure participation in the "Great Conversation that began in the dawn of history and that continues to the present day."[29] *Great Books of the Western World* was a large-scale commercial enterprise, a new version of Eliot's five-foot shelf under the imprint of the *Encyclopaedia Britannica*, with Adler as associate editor and John Erskine, by then in his seventies, on its advisory board. As one of Hutchins's biographers observes, the project capitalized and copyrighted "Great Books."[30] Hutchins's utopian hopes and their subsequent commercial redaction, however one may estimate the value of either, gave a presumptive value to "great books" that the aestheticism of Woodberry or Erskine could not reach. Like the institution of "the humanities," that of "great books," especially as Hutchins represented, capitalized, and copyrighted it, created new value in the marketplace.

What is more, as has become definitive for the curricular tradition of "Western Civilization," Hutchins's (and the *Encyclopaedia Britannica*'s) vision merged the history of Western civilization with that of its great books, a textual takeover of history that historians do not always accept gladly. In this vision, "literature" and the "great conversation" define Western history as well as Western civilization:

> The Western ideal is not one or the other strand in the Conversation, but the Conversation itself. It would be an exaggeration to say that Western civilization means these books [though only because the arts and music are omitted]. . . . But to the extent to which books can present the idea of a civilization, the idea of Western civilization is here presented. These books are the means of understanding our society and ourselves. They contain the great ideas that dominate us without our knowing it. There is no comparable repository of our tradition.[31]

Hutchins's belief still inspires those who look back to a lost age of intellectual consensus. When Allan Bloom, who taught at the University of Chicago, called for a return to "the good old Great Books approach" (despite a remarkably thorough and revelatory inventory of its shortcomings), he meant an approach that defines history as mediated and created through its texts.[32]

If one longs for order, it is not entirely foolish to long for some things as they were between the wars and just after, even conceding that the Woodberry-Erskine cult of "great books" carries some inexcusable associations. And yet, what is it that the nostalgists (such a word is needed badly enough to justify a neologism) are nostalgic for? With "neo-humanism," "great books," and "the humanities," with "Contemporary Civilization," "Problems of Citizenship," and "Western Civilization," the years between the wars produced in the curriculum a pastiche of aspirations to order. But only a pastiche. And rather than yielding a consensus immune to the intellectual and social ferment of the latter half of the century, it may have helped generate the further instabilities that were to come. What is most important about the years between the wars is not that they produced true consensus but that they did not.

VII

General Education 'in a Free Society'

*Harvard's Redbook, the '1960s,'
and the Image of Democracy*

Charles Eliot, James McCosh, Charles Francis Adams, Charles Homer Haskins, Irving Babbitt, even George Edward Woodberry and John Erskine, and certainly Robert Maynard Hutchins, all these are familiar names. Harry D. Gideonse, who along with John Dewey and others criticized Hutchins's vision of a university based on an overriding metaphysics, is less well known, yet since Eliot no one has challenged the idea of a set curriculum more trenchantly. A native of Rotterdam, with an undergraduate degree from Columbia and a doctorate in economics from Geneva, and later to become president of Brooklyn College, Gideonse was an associate professor of economics at Chicago and chairman of "Social Sciences Courses in the College" when Hutchins published a book with the same title as that of Thorstein Veblen published two decades earlier—but with a message very different from Veblen's "memorandum on the conduct of universities by business men": *The Higher Learning in America* (1936). Gideonse responded to Hutchins with *The Higher Learning in a Democracy: A Reply to Presi-*

dent Hutchins' Critique of the American University (1937), a 34-page pamphlet that, in its focus on the elemental conditions of democracy, could be said to have set the stage for the less tempered critiques of an imposed centrality that later ushered in a new revolution. Gideonse brought to his task the indignation of an insider, a European sensibility, and a judicious steering clear of views that might have seemed to reflect too directly his profession as an economist.

Hutchins's book and Gideonse's pamphlet, the one about learning "in America" and the other about learning "in a democracy," clash in their understanding of higher learning and its contexts. When Hutchins names his subject "the higher learning in America," he means something largely independent of its social environment, an ideal value that in America is not achieved. When Gideonse names his subject "the higher learning in a democracy," he refers to a value that can only be captured, acted on, and understood in its particular context: what will (or should) higher learning be like in a democracy? In the one case, education is a transcultural ideal; in the other, it is contingent. In this, Hutchins is the ancient, Gideonse the modern. Yet phrases like "the higher learning in" are likely in every case to straddle the ideal and the contingent: there can be more (in Gideonse's case) or very much less (in Hutchins's) of a relationship between the social context and the character of education, but there cannot be no relation at all; nor can the "higher" learning or any form of education ever be stripped of claims to value. Therefore the issue is, how well worked out is the relationship between an educational agenda and the social structure—or individual university—within which it operates or is proposed? This question has practical consequences, as in Harvard's famous Redbook, otherwise called *General Education in a Free Society* (1945), or in the ten-part *Study of Education at Stanford* (1968)—both of them documents in which the problem of that relationship is blurred. Gideonse, to the contrary, highlights it.

The "confusion" and "disorder" that Hutchins finds intolerable, Gideonse regards not only as inevitable but as the not undesirable consequence of attempts to get at truth: "The unfettered competition of truths—which is 'confusing' and 'disorderly'—is at the same time the very essence of a democratic society. Democracy is a plant that must be cultivated; only a continuous tolerance of and vigilant care for variety will preserve and extend our heritage. To crystallize truths into Truth and to substitute metaphysics for science is to arrest a process of intellectual growth that is the basis of the democratic process." Above all, Hutchins is wrong to believe that no essential difference distinguishes intellectual virtues in democracies, aristocracies, oligarchies, or monarchies, and in this he radically undervalues education's social determinants. Instead of the "Truth enshrined in Books" (the uppercase letter anticipates ironically the later commercial flowering of "great books" into "Great Books"), modern education should emphasize "the method of science" and, as William Hamilton had argued a century earlier, stress ways by which "new truth is established and ancient truths are corrected."[1] Mortimer Adler is said to have sent Hutchins a "prolix" commentary on *The Higher Learning in a Democracy*, along with exhortations "to correct them"— that is, the opposition—"all along the line on their bad intellectual history."[2] But a thinker less dogmatic than Adler might have conceded the importance of social context without giving up the right to disagree about the content of education in a democracy.

Since "Contemporary Civilization" came to Columbia, American higher education has puzzled repeatedly over the venerable question, what consequences follow for the curriculum "in a democracy?" After the war, Harvard took up the question in its Redbook, a study initiated by President James Bryant Conant and, in the event, an enterprise remarkable for its ambition and attempt at outreach. Those consulted by the committee included Reinhold Niebuhr, a representative of the

International Ladies' Garment Workers Union, the commissioner of education of the state of New York, the supervisor of "Employment and Services" for the International Harvester Company, and others on a list over two pages long—a list surely influenced by the mandate to study general education "in a free society." For all this apparatus of consultation, however, the outcome of the enterprise (with hindsight) looks like a beginning of an end to the aspirations to order that had flowered before the war. For the committee's most rigorous proposals, namely, for required courses in humanities, social sciences, and natural sciences, were not put in effect: a vote of the faculty, 135 to 10, approved the committee report in principle but with the large exception that no fewer than two nor more than four alternative courses be offered in each of the three areas.[3] Unquestionably the original proposal went too far, thereby exposing inescapable limits to consensus, prescription, and indeed practicality: the proposal would not have been easy to implement. But above all it rubbed against the grain of a university that had become what it was in the days of Charles Eliot, and against the grain of a society in which aspirations to order soon run up against, in fact stimulate, competing demands of freedom and election. Harvard's decision ensured that the American curriculum would continue to be defined more by heterogeneity than by uniformity. Limits had been tested, and a recognition of realities, unwelcome to some, had prevailed.

There are other reasons, however, more exact than that of going "too far" and visible in retrospect, why so grand an effort did not carry full conviction. In the first place, the Redbook is curiously airless, marked by an inability to see much beyond the boundaries of Cambridge or to achieve historical perspective despite its huge apparatus of consultation. Except for passing references, including one to "the authoritative figure of President Eliot," the report reads as if American education had no history.[4] In the second place, and partly as a consequence, the report lacks originality. In the third place, the failure to see much beyond the boundaries of Cambridge almost assured that the relationship between local conditions and the needs of a "free society" would be, as it is, unsatisfactorily defined. In this, the Redbook may be our most instructive, cautionary example of how not to try to have it, in matters of curricular prescription, both ways; that is, how not to mix up claims of the local and of the universal. In these several respects, this influential document—influential at least in its large number of printings—displays many of the habits that have handicapped debates in American higher education.

Were it not endemic, the Redbook's lack of historical perspective would be surprising coming from a committee dominated by historians, with Paul Buck as chairman and, among the members, Arthur M. Schlesinger, Sr., and others of a historical cast of mind. Early in the report the committee alludes to the threefold division of knowledge—"Tradition points to a separation of learning into the three areas of natural science, social studies, and the humanities"[5]—without noticing the relative newness of the taxonomy. And were it not for Harvard's habitual isolation (until recently), the faint attention paid to reforms at Columbia and Chicago before the war would be equally surprising. In *The Reforming of General Education: The Columbia College Experience in Its National Setting* (1966), which in its subtitle skirts the problem of education at Columbia as related to education at large, Daniel Bell raised an eyebrow at Harvard's performance—"Why there should have been such parochialism is difficult to understand"—though he surely understood the reasons quite well.[6] The consequence of this parochialism was that Harvard, while seeming to preach a new religion, reproduced attitudes and beliefs that had flourished, though unevenly, since Eliot's presidency ended in 1909.

Of the courses it proposed, the committee suggested that one in the humanities "might be called 'Great Texts of Literature.'" Another in the "social sciences"—no longer "social studies," as earlier in the report, a change probably stemming from a belated desire to dignify what might otherwise too much recall the high school curriculum—"might be called 'Western Thought and Institutions'" but *not* "The Evolution of Free Society," lest the title carry "implications of indoctrination which would be unacceptable to many."[7] And in the sciences a course in the principles either of physics or biology would be required. Except for the science requirement, something Columbia had talked about but not implemented, little is new.

Just how little is clear from the readings suggested for "Great Texts" and for "Western Thought and Institutions." For the first, Homer, one or two Greek tragedies, Plato, the Bible, Virgil, Dante, Shakespeare, Milton, Tolstoy. For the second, Plato and Aristotle and, after them, Aquinas, Machiavelli, Luther, Bodin, Locke, Montesquieu, Rousseau, Adam Smith, Bentham, Mill, all of them offering "materials admirably suited to serve the purpose of such a course." The open-eyed air of discovery comes with an afterthought and a disingenuous double negative: "The course is not unlike the very successful introductory course, 'Contemporary Civilization,' which has been given at Columbia during the past twenty-six years"—although the report suggests, in Cantabrigian fashion, "that it would be preferable to deal with fewer topics and to read longer portions of fewer books than has been customary in that admirable course." Seldom has such an effort, two years in the process, been devoted to reinventing the wheel.[8]

These difficulties are all connected with the failure to settle the relationship between local and national interest. On the one hand, the report considers "general education in a free society" and opens with reflections on "two characteristic facets of democracy: the one, its creativity, sprung from the self-trust of its members; the other, its exposure to discord and even to fundamental divergence of standards precisely because of this creativity, the source of its strength." On the other hand, the report stresses the "enormous diversity" of American higher education, criticizes those who approach educational problems "as though the term, college, had a single specific meaning throughout the United States," and insists that its proposals are for Harvard alone: "Harvard's present structure and condition is the ground on which we must build, the context within which we must plan."[9]

Of course Harvard could not easily present its recommendations as a nostrum for all. But the report fails to establish how the proposals are fitted to a unique or even a very unusual set of local circumstances, and the classicist E. K. Rand chided the committee for not more bravely sticking to its guns and recommending a program "for all our liberal colleges" (while at the same time he urged less prescription and more election).[10] It is hardly enough to point out, as a mark of singularity, "a most important consideration, Harvard's present size. It is a large institution, and it is one part of a much larger university"; or that Harvard draws its students from all over and from different backgrounds.[11] Though Harvard led some other universities in the catholicity of its student population, its size and diversity both reflect ongoing tendencies of American higher education after the war. Consequently, what Harvard could not say out loud, namely, that it was proposing a generic program, got said obliquely. *General Education in a Free Society*, in trying to avoid the imperial ambitions of a Hutchins, never achieves the contextual concentration of a Gideonse. Had its recommendations been adopted, however, and had the results been even temporarily successful, Charles Eliot's idea of a university would have been compromised at Harvard more thoroughly than ever before. And other institutions would probably have followed suit.

If all that had happened, the Redbook might have seemed less parochial than prophetic, and Columbia's two required courses, one of them long in the creation, might have seemed a preliminary experiment that Harvard bravely pressed to its conclusion. But even if the Redbook had carried more conviction and if its requirements had been put in place, history was conspiring to make certain they would have come under fire quite soon. Under the cultural pressures of the cold war, instability threatened, earlier indeed than is usually remembered in accounts of "the 1960s." And by putting Western institutions into jeopardy, these pressures also put courses on Western thought and its institutions under threat.

Against the recommendations, preoccupations, and attitudes of the Redbook may be set a fugitive journalistic exercise, long forgotten except by a few who were on the scene, that appeared in June 1956. This was a special issue of *i.e.: The Cambridge Review*, a journal that survived for six numbers in 1955–56. If the Redbook offered recommendations that exposed the limits of prescription, *Harvard: 1956*, as this special issue was called, has the retrospective look of prophecy, for in it the 1960s and their discontents are foreshadowed. The Redbook turned out to show what could not be done; *Harvard: 1956* showed the way to a future in which prescription of any sort came under suspicion—as it had (however different the reasons) in the Harvard of Charles Eliot.

The co-authors of *Harvard: 1956* were four students, one a fourth-year Ph.D. candidate in English, two seniors, and one junior—the first time in this narrative that students have played a part, surprisingly so because the disruptive, even rebellious presence of students was common in the earlier history of universities. Seldom have students been so passive as in the American university of the early and mid–twentieth century. It is as if energies long under restraint were finally released in the 1960s, and students' continuing involvement in curricular (and other) questions since then is not aberrant. On the contrary, it is business as usual or business as it once was. Forgotten though it is, *Harvard: 1956* was a distant early warning of what was coming. In some future history of Harvard, it could play a role like that, in Samuel Eliot Morison's account, of "A True Description of A Number of tyrannical Pedagogues"—a mock-heroic poem dedicated to the "Sons of H*****D" and published in 1769 as liberty was stirring in the colonies.[12] Students are adept at catching whatever mood is "in the air"; it is, after all, in part their own creation.

Though *Harvard: 1956* offers no systematic treatment of curricular questions, it touches on them. The authors have some good things to say about the new introductory courses in general education, the basis of distribution requirements that were the chief product of the Redbook's recommendations ("They are anti-scholarly in a good sense"), and some bad things also ("Undoubtedly the student does learn a technique, but a good percentage of this technique is fraud. That is, the student does not understand what he is doing.") But behind these casual views lie deeper yearnings, in the face of dangers that threatened mass destruction, for a wholesale unmaking of the system.[13]

These yearnings express themselves as a desire for greater freedom, especially sexual freedom; as a desire for a more caring world; and as a latent fear of, mixed with the desire for, apocalypse. Wishing to be left alone yet wishing to be cared for and half-wishing for the violence of an ending, the authors sketch a psychological agenda for the decade ahead. On that agenda the structure of the traditional curriculum would be more central than could have been guessed in 1956.

"Above all, liberate your responses." This rallying call comes with a gloss that, as a clue to understanding, matters more than the message: "Above all, liberate your responses, if they still exist. If they do not, then the most important move towards the machine of destruction has been taken. And perhaps historically it is our civilization's task to pave the way for the atom bomb—to finish passively a destruction that started long ago." In such an environment, repression is the enemy, and at its most daring, *Harvard: 1956* calls for a new relationship between faculty and students: "Tutors and professors, if they are to live, must be involved with their students, even in a latently sexual manner, with the possibility of the sex becoming overt. You cannot have creative latent sexuality (in this case it would necessarily often be latent homosexuality) without admitting the possibility of its being overt." But sexuality in the long run is less the real issue than authority and the idea of authority, and behind it all lies the desire to call an end to a received version of "civilization." Having brought its own survival into question with engines of destruction, Western civilization—and therefore "Western Civilization," the curricular jewel in the crown of the American academy (if not at Harvard)—begin to look like ghosts of an illusory past.[14]

When the ambiguous yearnings reflected in *Harvard: 1956* were exposed to the experience of the 1960s, it was Stanford—brash, energetic, Western, naive—that most eagerly took up the new educational agenda. In 1967, President J. E. Wallace Sterling appointed a steering committee that late in 1968 published the ten-part *Study of Education at Stanford*. Like other institutions, universities tend to repeat their own histories, and the steering committee seems as oddly constituted for its task as the Cathcart committee had been almost five decades earlier. Chairing the study was a distinguished lawyer, Herbert L. Packer, then vice provost and a powerful figure in the community. Other faculty came from electrical engineering, psychology, genetics, and physics, all of them, like Packer, with big-league reputations. They were joined by an associate professor of history and three students, one a graduate student in physics, another in medicine, and an undergraduate in philosophy. It was this committee, with the assistance of "over 200 faculty members, staff members, and students" on a variety of subcommittees, that would echo, though without apparently knowing it, the doctrines of Charles Eliot, almost a hundred years precisely after Eliot became president of Harvard: "The faculty member should be free to pursue his intellectual interests wherever they lead him. The student, other things being equal, should be similarly free."[15]

Other things, the committee concedes, will not be equal,

but little separates its position from one that Arnold described caustically in 1865: "Our prevalent notion is . . . that it is a most happy and important thing for a man merely to be able to do as he likes. On what he is to do when he is thus free to do as he likes, we do not lay so much stress."[16] The committee did not go so far as to say to students, do what you like, but it pronounced the death of general education—"The general education ideal is totally impracticable as a dominant curricular pattern in the modern university"—and along with it, again in the name of freedom, went "Western Civilization," Stanford's flagship course for over 30 years: "Let the objective of curricular planning be to encourage the faculty member to teach what he likes to teach and the student to learn what seems vital to him—the Intellectual History of Europe in the Nineteenth Century rather than the History of Western Civilization . . ."[17]

In place of the old requirement would be a much vaguer one, a "one-semester course," any course, "in historical studies." What constituted "historical studies" the committee was unprepared to say, but it found "suggestive" a definition proposed by another committee on undergraduate education: a course in historical studies would "place emphasis upon the varied relationships existing between such aspects of a society's life as its political and administrative institutions, its system of class stratification, its material means of production, its intellectual and cultural activities, and the aspirations of its members, *and* upon the manner in which these relationships are affected by the reciprocal operation of change and continuity." It is a definition of historical studies with much of the history, as usually understood, taken out and a new ideology put in. The recommendation was never implemented.[18]

In 1982, Gilbert Allardyce published a good essay titled "The Rise and Fall of the Western Civilization Course." It opens with Haskins's words to the American Historical Association in 1905, brings the story up through the revolution of the 1960s— "When compulsion stopped, enrollment dwindled, and across the nation, one after the other, Western Civ courses were decommissioned like old battleships"—and notices the onset of Thermidor, the moderating response to the curricular Terror of the late 1960s, a response discernible by the mid-1970s, when the Vietnam War was over. At the same time, Allardyce brings his narrative only to 1976, and even by 1982 it would have been hard fully to interpret the story or to predict the final destiny of "Western Civ." In one sense, however, Allardyce got it dead right: "Nostalgia is likely to remain."[19]

Allardyce only underestimated the depth and strength of that nostalgia. He also said, "Most historians have long concluded that the world has outgrown the old Western Civ ideas," and in this he underestimated not only the power of nostalgia but the difficulties of keeping a steady course in stormy intellectual and political seas.[20] The nostalgia induced by the decline and fall of "Western Civilization"—and the associated decline and fall of "great books," with which "Western Civilization" since Hutchins had been intimately associated—produced the strange, sometimes almost comic, events of the last decade, puzzling at first glance but fitting the pattern, long in the making, of cyclical alternation and intermittent change in the forms of liberal education. By the time of Allardyce's essay, Stanford had already (in 1980) revived "Western Civilization" as "Western Culture," a new name full of resonance and, also, of unanticipated dangers.

VIII

Orbs, Epicycles, and the Wars of 'Culture'

According to media (and other) accounts, Stanford in the late 1980s took a step of unparalleled extremity and daring, repudiating long-shared beliefs in "the canon" of Western civilization (or Western culture) that provided the solid ground of American higher education. In the late 1980s, legend has it, Stanford rejected the Western "heritage." Others have pointed out distortions in the legend, yet it can hardly be emphasized strenuously enough or often enough how far from truth and into demagoguery the legend strays, so fragile, partial, and short-lived was any prior consensus.

Furthermore, Stanford was suffering from its good intentions and from a decision in which even its opponents could have found at least limited merit: that is, the effort to reconstruct early in the 1980s what it had given up only a decade before, namely, a freshman requirement based on a common reading list—the very reading list that would become, in the next upheaval, the source of so much controversy. In making its complete—or almost complete—about-face early in the 1980s, Stanford may have been unique among American universities, but it moved in accord with a counter-revolutionary spirit of the day. If it turns out, however, that this Thermidorian reaction to the 1960s' revolution was just an interlude in a process that reconfigures the curriculum, some weight will rest on the decision to replace the old "Western Civilization" not with a new "Western Civilization" but with "Western Culture." For if fundamental reconfiguration comes, it will almost surely come through new understandings of "culture." In that event, to resurrect the image that McCosh used in 1885, Stanford's effort to hang onto older values will look like a case of trying to preserve a Ptolemaic universe when a Copernican alternative had already made irreversible gains. The requirement in "Western Culture" was an intricate contraption of cycle and epicycle, orb in orb.

In the first place, the requirement returned to the curriculum as one (the first) among eight distribution requirements. In the second place, it aimed to marry the unity of a common set of texts to a variety of "tracks," a marriage of considerable inconvenience to some of the participants. The "tracks" in "Western Culture" included "Great Works of Western Culture," "Western Thought and Literature," "Ideas in Western Culture," "Europe: From the Middle Ages to the Present," "Western Culture and Technology," and a few more. "Great Works of Western Culture," by its nature, avoided the awkwardness of fitting fixed texts to a supervening theme; and so, largely, did "Western Thought and Literature," a course that had been offered for nearly 40 years under the auspices of what were known as "Humanities Special Programs." But how (in practice) might (or should) the courses differ? And how would a "track" in comparative literature distinguish its offering? Comparative literature's solution—imposing a taxonomy independent of chronology ("The Literature of Interaction and Conflict," "The Literature of Introspection," "The Literature of Speculation") —seemed intellectually fragile to at least one of those (myself) who taught in the "track"; and its limitation of enrollment to twenty students, however desirable in theory, in practice put the offering at odds with the larger environment (as programs in comparative literature tend to be).

More difficult still, what could "Western Culture and Technology" do with, say, Augustine's *Confessions*? Not an impossible question—Augustine's conversion came in an encounter with the written word and, as one of the instructors who labored under the difficulty remarks, "There is probably no book in the canon that is not so protean that it cannot be 'mined' for its possible bearing on technology (or God, or social change, or any other grand theme)"—but having to find an answer underscored the compromises on which the new system was based.[1] In its pluralism (the more "Western Cultures," the better), the system defied easy explanation, courted further instability, and exposed it to the uproar later in the decade when the common reading list of fifteen required and some other "strongly recommended" texts was supplanted by an annual list of six texts or authors, a change leading to the repeated assertions that Stanford was destroying "Western Civilization"—and Western civilization.

Despite the national commotion, anyone looking at Stanford's listing of courses and degrees before and after the sea change of the late 1980s would detect only ripples. The requirement is no longer "Western Culture" but "Cultures, Ideas, and Values." A new track called "Europe and the Americas" (which in its subject matter provoked the *Wall Street Journal* to editorial outrage and provided Dinesh D'Souza with material for a chapter of his *Illiberal Education* [1991]) is now among the options. That the list of shared texts, never spelled out in the catalogue, has been redrawn cannot be inferred, reasonably enough because from the beginning the important thing has been that some set of readings, but not an immutable list, should be shared. The continuity of the entry before and after the revision appears to mark a modest epicyclical adjustment after two years of bitter infighting.

Yet something considerable has happened, most visibly in the program's new name, "Cultures, Ideas, and Values," a change that, like the shift from "Western Civilization" to "Western

Culture," may also be seen some day as signaling a new Copernican universe. If so, the political authorities who fought the change, like religious authorities of the earlier time, were right to think that the intellectual framework of their own system, hence its existence, was at risk. Competing meanings of "culture" have been a spectral presence throughout this narrative, and, like Hamlet's father's ghost, here they arrive suddenly on stage, together with the gathering claims of a discipline other than history or literature to the intellectual action—namely, cultural anthropology.

An upstart discipline (though in some respects as old as mind itself), anthropology as the study of cultures became a coherent enterprise long after literature, history, or philosophy, achieving new shape and definition at the end of the nineteenth century, almost simultaneously with Arnold's celebration of high culture. The changing title of Stanford's required course over seven decades of interrupted existence amounts to a gradual triumph of the anthropological: first, "Problems of Citizenship," a dressed-up version of "civics"; then "Western Civilization," implying the Arnoldian dream of a perfected, high civilization; then "Western Culture," leaving the meaning of "Culture"— whether entailing a positive judgment or a more neutral treatment of Western experience—partly to the taste of the observer; and, finally (so far), "Cultures, Ideas, and Values," with its implication that ideas are open to anthropological scrutiny and that "ideas" and "values" are culturally derived. That "Cultures, Ideas, and Values" can be abbreviated to the acronym "CIV" is a calculated, Ptolemaic ambivalence, one more symptom of hanging on, however precariously, to a threatened and perhaps vanishing past.

Since Edward Tylor, whose *Primitive Culture* (1871) put the discipline on a firm footing, the history of cultural anthropology is that of evolutionary theories being replaced by resistance, derived from philosophers of the Enlightenment and owing above all in the anthropological setting to Franz Boas, to cultural ethnocentrism and to accounts of "primitive" societies as gradually ascending a neo-Darwinian chain of being. Yet even the evolutionary theories of Tylor or of the American anthropologist Lewis Henry Morgan, whose *magnum opus* was *Ancient Society or Researches in the Lines of Human Progress from Savagery Through Barbarism to Civilization* (1877), endow early society and its culture with a value unthinkable in Arnold's account. The early anthropologists proposed a model in which "the best that has been known and said in the world" comprises only a tiny fraction of human experience and perhaps not the most important part at that. Arnold's universe was "Ptolemaic": at its center was the best that had been known and said. That of Tylor and Morgan was "Copernican," or proto-Copernican, on its way to displacing high culture from a situation of exclusive privilege. That these antithetical models have existed side by side for a hundred years is unsurprising. The Copernican universe prevailed only gradually. In 1667, some 130 years after Copernicus had made his theory known to the world, Milton used the Ptolemaic system for the cosmology of *Paradise Lost*. If what we are watching is the gradual triumph of the anthropological, it is natural that the change should be slow and contested all the way.

Since 1933, the title of Tylor's pathbreaking study has appeared in the *Oxford English Dictionary* as the second instance (the first, dating from 1867, comes from Edward Augustus Freeman's *History of the Norman Conquest*) of "culture" as signifying the whole fabric of a society. And Tylor's famous first sentence announces a semiotics of culture, "in its wide ethnographic sense," that not only can be regarded as a counterstatement to Arnold but in the view of George Stocking was so intended by its author: "Culture or Civilization, taken in its wide ethnographic sense, is that complex whole which includes knowledge, belief, art, morals, law, custom, and any other capabilities and habits acquired by man as a member of society." Whatever exactly it may be, "culture" incorporates a society's ideas and values.[2]

And, even granting that Tylor as much as Arnold thought in terms of high civilizations and low, the recognition that the "advance of culture" is an up-and-down affair colors Tylor's account of civilization's progress: "Whether in high ranges or in low of human life, it may be seen that advance of culture seldom results at once in unmixed good." This is especially true of colonialism: "The white invader or colonist, though representing on the whole a higher moral standard than the savage he improves or destroys, often represents his standard very ill, and at best can hardly claim to substitute a life stronger, nobler, and purer at every point than that which he supersedes." Tylor believes more firmly than some would now that "any known savage tribe would . . . be improved by judicious civilization," but his argument weighs against extremes of ethnocentricity.[3]

From its beginning in Tylor to the present, the anthropological impulse has set itself, whether obliquely or squarely, against the exclusionary dogma of high culture and thus altered the intellectual terrain. If Stocking is right that in *Primitive Culture* Tylor intended specifically to amend Arnold, then Tylor can be said to have taken "the contemporary humanist idea of culture and fitted it into the framework of progressive social evolutionism. One might say he made Matthew Arnold's culture evolutionary. To do so was no small contribution."[4]

For Morgan, the hypothesis of social evolution precludes a belief in some ur-civilization, Hebrew or Roman, as having set a standard from which tribal societies have fallen away.[5] And for Boas, taking matters a step further, "it is somewhat difficult for us to recognize that the value which we attribute to our own civilization is due to the fact that we participate in this civilization, and that it has been controlling all our actions since the time of our birth." Therefore, "it is certainly conceivable that there may be other civilizations . . . which are of no less value than ours." Having become a full professor at Columbia in 1899, Boas published the first edition of *The Mind of Primitive Man* (from which the preceding excerpt comes) in 1911, in it rejecting the belief in linear progress, addressing, in its final chapter, the "race problem in modern society," and dismissing the claim— represented most offensively by the likes of Henry F. Suksdorf, whose *Our Race Problems* was published in the same year—that "race determines culture."[6]

Just as Tylor was contemporaneous with Arnold, Boas was contemporaneous with Woodberry and Erskine, Arnold's great-books devotees at Columbia, and for a time Boas's career also overlapped that of their more sophisticated successor Lionel Trilling. But the name of the European-born Boas never became so nearly synonymous as that of Woodberry or Erskine or Trilling with the genius of the place. In the bicentennial history of Columbia College, Trilling contributes a historical essay, and Woodberry and Erskine share places of honor. Lacking their institutional influence, Boas is never mentioned.[7] Notwithstanding Boas's concern for his own (adopted) American scene, anthropologists for a long time were thought of, and often thought of themselves, as concerned only with other societies "out there." The two cultures of "great books" and anthropology looked past each other. Not yet were they on a collision—or even on a convergent—course.

Of course it simplifies matters to suppose that anthropology —a sophisticated intellectual discipline—can be presentably characterized in monochrome. In "Culture, Genuine and Spurious" (1924), Edward Sapir, often thought the most brilliant of American anthropologists, set out his "idea of what kind of a good thing culture is" and defined its character, whether in the West, in Islamic polygamous societies, or in American Indian non-agricultural societies—that is, across the spectrum of human differences—as including harmony, balance, and "a richly varied and yet somehow unified and consistent attitude toward life."[8] An ideal difficult of measurement, no doubt, but an ideal nonetheless.

And, after the Second World War, accounts that asserted (or seemed to) a relativity of cultural value were subject to humanistic critiques by anthropologists, critiques parallel in motive to those of the curricular revisionism that followed both wars. In 1953 Robert Redfield, then the Robert Maynard Hutchins Distinguished Service Professor at the University of Chicago and an anthropologist of the first rank, wrote in *The Primitive World and Its Transformations*, originally presented as lectures at Cornell: "I am persuaded that cultural relativism is in for some difficult times." This was almost a self-fulfilling prophecy, given his own analysis: "It was easy to look with equal benevolence upon all sorts of value systems so long as the values were those of unimportant little people remote from our own concerns. But the equal benevolence is harder to maintain when one is asked to anthropologize the Nazis."[9] In the recoil from atrocity and genocide, anthropologizing the Nazis seemed beyond the usual instruments and attitudes of the discipline as well as beyond ordinary human understanding.

An even more strenuous critic of cultural relativism, and one who also drew intellectual capital from the example of the war, was the maverick David Bidney, whose career began with a Yale dissertation on Spinoza. In 1950 Bidney went to the University of Indiana, with a joint appointment in philosophy and anthropology, and there for almost three decades introduced his anthropology students to Locke and Kant, Dewey and James. In 1953, the same year as Redfield's *The Primitive World and Its Transformations*, Bidney attacked cultural relativism— and the American anthropological tradition generally—in an article called "The Concept of Value in Modern Anthropology." What was largely implicit in Columbia's creation of "Contemporary Civilization" after the first war or in Harvard's Redbook after the second stands out vividly in Bidney's commentary on

Boas and democratic liberalism, a commentary recalling Babbitt on Rousseau and Romantic primitivism: "In retrospect,
it appears that American anthropologists continued to reflect
the prevailing attitude of their democratic society. As liberals
and democrats they merely accentuated tendencies inherent in
their culture but professed to have derived their 'higher tolerance' from a comparative study of primitive cultures." Boas's
ideology, that is, precedes rather than follows from his analysis of culture. Had anthropologists only "thought in terms of
the possible incompatibility and conflict of ideologies and of
the doctrine of social revolution rather than of social evolution, they would not have labored under the naïve optimism
of cultural laissez faire. It has taken the impact of the second
World War to shake this romantic cultural optimism."[10] And
in a chapter of his *Theoretical Anthropology*, also published in
1953, Bidney argued for "a normative science of culture" that
would formulate "cultural ideals as possible means and ends of
sociocultural life." Only such a normative science could steer
between the extremes of Nazism and Communism, since "only
a cultural unity based upon a common core of rational values
and brought into being by voluntary deliberate consent can en-
dure indefinitely."[11] But no normative science of culture was in
the cards. Revisionist anthropology never seriously upset the
dominance of Boas and his followers, however much it may
have added to the self-understanding of the anthropological
calling.

One source of Redfield's and Bidney's discomfort may have
been that by 1953, the dominant relativism of anthropology had
already begun to infiltrate the heart of the curriculum, even
in circumstances and places that might be thought inhospit-
able. If the Redbook in fact sought to sponsor an educated
cultural consensus based on Western traditions, then considerable irony attaches to the pervasiveness and popularity of Ruth
Benedict's *Patterns of Culture* (1934) at postwar Harvard. Benedict's book, Bidney wrote, "gave articulate expression to the

accepted ethnological mode of thinking" and, in particular, to
the belief that "the abnormal is only that which is divergent
from the cultural pattern of the community."[12] Although the
full extent of Benedict's influence on the Harvard curriculum
is hard to reconstruct, *Patterns of Culture* (at a cost of 35 cents
for a paperback) was assigned in at least three general education courses in social science; and I know I am not wrong in
remembering that discovering *Patterns of Culture*, with its resistance to the ethnocentric habit of identifying "our local ways
of behaving with Behaviour, or our own socialized habits with
Human Nature," was something of an initiation rite (and a welcome one) to Harvard undergraduates of the early 1950s.[13] If
proponents of "great books" and "Western Civilization" need
evidence of intellectual subversion in the university curriculum,
they should look farther back than Stanford in the 1980s and
farther back even than disruptions of the 1960s. Subversion was
abroad in Cambridge by 1949.

To the subtle encroachment of the anthropological should
be added the less subtle influence of "cultural studies" as de-
scended from the work of the Welsh-born, Cambridge-educated
Raymond Williams, whose *Culture and Society* (1958), without
ever referring to the anthropological tradition of Tylor and
Boas, set the stage for an extension of that tradition to incorporate a Marxist ethics. Mass culture, according to Williams, is
not the merely tawdry thing that apostles of high culture, like
his Cambridge contemporary F. R. Leavis, claim. Rather, it is
"the culture of the disinherited," and Williams looks ahead to
a time when a new, collective, open culture will be formed on
the wreckage of the old.[14] Mass culture, however mixed its aspect, depends in part on human needs that are more authentic
not than those of high culture itself but than those manifested
by certain of its acolytes: "The argument against these things,
and the immense profits gained by their calculated dissemina-
tion, cannot afford to be confused by the collateral point that a
good living culture is various and changing, that the need for

sport and entertainment is as real as the need for art, and that
the public display of 'taste' as a form of social distinction, is
merely vulgar."[15]

With the influence of Boas, "the epitome of the nineteenth-
century liberal," on one side;[16] that of Williams, the epitome
of the twentieth-century intellectual populist, on another; and
the residual influence of Arnold on yet another, the concept of
culture by the 1980s was both a site of contestation and a haven,
offering something for everyone. Its very ambiguity could be
construed as its salient virtue at a moment when traditional
categories of the human were in a state of disruption. This blurring of the conceptual field of culture mirrors what Clifford
Geertz described more than a decade ago as the blurring of
genres "in social science, as in intellectual life generally," which
in turn has entailed a blurring of terms—for example, "game,"
or "drama," or "text"—as one discipline appropriates the intellectual currency of another. "Cultures, Ideas, and Values," in
name if not yet in any finished shape, shares in Geertz's "refiguration of social thought."[17] Its terms are fluid, waiting to be
filled with experience and meaning.

Will this new requirement be as volatile as its predecessor,
"Western Culture?" On the answer hangs any future interpretation. Should the requirement remain in place for a decent
length of time, should it work its way into the minds of students anywhere near so deeply as "Western Civilization" did
during its 30-year run, and (above all) should it preserve a mea-
surable trace of "culture"'s Arnoldian meanings, that would
argue against the cosmological analogy. But if that analogy is
to the point—that is, if the new requirement reflects only a
Ptolemaic adjustment in the presence of a new Copernican system—then constant pressure on it should be predictable. Such
pressure seems to be building. To the distribution requirements
of which "Cultures, Ideas, and Values" makes one part, there
have been added components in "gender studies" and "American cultures." And in March 1992 the *Stanford Daily* reported

four new proposed "CIV" "tracks." One of these, its financially troubled sponsor, the Department of Drama, described as arising from "crass" motives: "It's for the money."[18] Future students of American education may find such incidental commentary almost as valuable to the task of understanding as the intellectual squabbles that attended the birth of "Cultures, Ideas, and Values."

IX

What to Do?

The title of this section is misleading, if it be taken as announcing some new curriculum. The more inclusive such proposals are, the less likely they are to carry weight. The best that can be done is to think about ways to think about the issues. Because there are no more Charles Eliots—that is to say, university presidents with the luxury of seriously attending to curricular questions or who have sufficient influence with their faculties to generate consenting change; because committee members charged with curricular questions steal time from competing obligations; because academic senates meet intermittently and have inadequate time for deliberation; and because politicians are politicians, curricular questions have been handled with indifference masquerading as concern.

Only indifference and self-interest could account for the persistence, against all historical evidence, of the myth of untroubled consensus and precipitous decline in the condition of the curriculum. Is it too much to hope, with Irving Babbitt 80 years ago, that ancients and moderns might consent to a truce and concede that neither side benefits much from perpetuating a legend or the warfare that goes with it? Granted, the ancients seem to have the most to lose in a truce: their case has rested on a view of the moderns as subverting ancient verities. Yet the facts are so plain, and the ancients so little able to carry conviction amongst the moderns when their case is framed in generational and legendary terms, that a fair settlement might actually help breathe life into the cause of traditional humanism. If I am right that, for every Arnoldian on the barricades, two more Newmanians are working away in their library offices, a truce might draw some of the latter into the open air. If ordinary human reticence has accounted for a measure of their withdrawal, so has the unhelpful spectacle of thrust and counterthrust on behalf of causes not fully understood. A truce might create an arena in which more interested parties wished to participate. What the outcome would be is impossible to know, but it is far from certain that the setting aside of myth would leave the ancients at a greater disadvantage than they are at currently, when it comes not to scoring political points but to affecting decisions taken by university faculties. The ancients, that is, might even gain some political advantage by seeming, like the very modern Charles Eliot, to set political advantage aside.

Imagine, in any case, a situation in which higher education had finally moved beyond the antagonisms of ancients and moderns, and imagine then what kinds of empirical issues would rise to the surface. In the first place, the evidence of history could only become more welcome and more needful as legend receded into the background, and universities might better perceive the institutional uses of understanding their own past, of which they have been haphazard stewards. However ephemeral-seeming the contents of any single course, significance will often emerge at this level of detail—and the history of curricular change, merely by being understood, can have a formative influence on current practice. Stanford is lucky to have preserved in its archives extensive materials, including lectures, committee reports, minutes, and so forth, from which could be constructed a more detailed account of how "Problems of Citizenship" was created and how it evolved into "Western Civilization" than anything attempted in this book. Edgar Eugene Robinson's printed lecture of 1928, reproduced in an appendix here, is only a tiny fragment of what is available. Moreover, universities are beginning to realize that curricular records, far from being mere ephemera, represent the basis of what might not too extravagantly be thought of as a national *bildungsroman*. Columbia University has announced a program to gather whatever uncollected materials it can touching its core curriculum, a valuable effort and, one hopes, a sign of the times. The story of the American curriculum, too often neglected in the universities where it has been played out, may be coming into its own.

The university and its curriculum provide in fact as good an index as can be found to the nation's social and intellectual history. Veblen put it nicely in *The Higher Learning in America*: as an institution, the university is, like any other, "a prevalent habit of thought" and, as much as any other in this society, a place where values are created and enforced, challenged and sometimes changed.[1] When this is taken into account, the history of American higher education assumes new centrality. The relationship between "civics," "nativism," civic education in general, and the coming of "Western Civilization" courses becomes (for example) more recognizably what it is, an integral part of America's response to immigration, a response that has determined so much of our educational practice and (sometimes covertly) so many of our curricular skirmishes. That A. Lawrence Lowell, Eliot's successor, not only opposed free election but was a prominent member of the Immigration Restriction League becomes a clue to a network of social beliefs, affecting social practices, within American culture.

As an index of intellectual values, separate from though influenced by social values, the history of the curriculum might tell us much else, too. How exactly did the history of Western Civilization become, as it did with Hutchins, so closely identified with its texts, especially its "great" texts—and why? If the question is seldom asked, it is because the identification of history and its texts has become part of our normal thinking—and because written materials provide much of our access to history—but not because there is no other way to think about the mainstream of history. Such a major yet imperceptibly achieved consensus can only have come about as a confluence of powerful currents. In 1941, "Contemporary Civilization" at Columbia undertook to include original sources for the first time, the result of the university's successful experience in teaching difficult texts to freshmen in the newly required "Humanities A."[2] In the 1930s, the tradition of New Criticism took hold, with its concentration on the text and its demotion of biographical and other external evidence as a guide to interpretation. At the same time, traditional narrative forms—such as historians even more automatically than novelists had always used as their vehicle— were subjected to pressure by writers like Joyce. Through what association of forces, then, did the narrative of "Western Civilization" give way to the aggregation of its texts? What part in this shift did the habits of a material culture play?

However much may yet be done to excavate the foundations of our thinking about curricular questions, the exercise will remain "academic" unless it is also a stimulus to action, and truly constructive action cannot take place without, first, the unknotting of a tangled skein of purposes. Charles Wegener, a thoughtful student of liberal education in the American university, came close to throwing his hands up in despair: "liberal education," he said, is a term so overloaded with meanings "that it is a good question whether it should be retained."[3] Yet the big question is not the abstract ideal of liberal education and its derivative strategies but the specific purpose of whatever it is, educationally, that we are trying to do. What is any requirement, or set of requirements, actually for?

Granted, complaints about the uncertain rationale of education are nothing very new. When Thomas Henry Huxley gave an address to the South London Working Men's College in 1868 called "A Liberal Education; and Where to Find It," he lamented, much as I am doing here, "the ravelled skeins" of thought on "the why and the wherefore of education."[4] Granted, also, it is sometimes easier to get things done without lingering over reasons. When the Harvard faculty, in the late 1970s, debated whether to institute what Henry Rosovsky called, astutely but not quite accurately, a "core curriculum," Samuel Beer, professor of government and a veteran of the Redbook days, stated the difficulty elegantly: as a young faculty member at the time of the Redbook, he said, he had "understood enough about such matters . . . to recognize that when a faculty discusses something like the rationale of education nothing was likely to happen, since any body, not normally organized into parties, customarily produced a negative majority against every meaningful proposition."[5] Beer was not arguing against but in favor of Rosovsky's core curriculum as an idea whose time had come at least to be tested. Yet what made Rosovsky's proposal appealing, if not proof against the possibility of a negative majority, was that it laid out in detail a rationale for the new curriculum, which was in effect a rearranged set of distribution requirements. Debates about the rationale of education risk futility. But the danger of proceeding with little serious rationale at all is greater. In academic as in other institutional settings, compromise usually comes in time. It is wiser to understand what is at stake than not to.

Distribution requirements, like Harvard's, have the advantage of at least one noncontroversial, self-evident function, namely that of acquainting students with the variety of knowledge. They also have the advantage, generally, of blending choice and prescription. Since Charles Eliot, few if any will be found to argue for entirely free election: American students do not know enough when they enter the university (it is agreed) to justify it. The noncontroversial basis of "distribution" accounts for the shape of some recent exercises in educational reform. Harvard revised its distribution requirements and called the result a "core curriculum," while Stanford softened the edge of its mandatory course not only by placing emphasis on a commonalty of reading in a choice of several tracks but also by construing "Western Culture" and then "Cultures, Ideas, and Values" as *primus inter pares* in its set of distribution requirements. But as Stanford discovered, whatever its countermeasures, when a single course, or even the choice among several trying to pass as one, is required, there is no avoiding the appearance—therefore, indeed, the reality—of having mandated the one thing needful and creating a stage where conflicts of purpose and value are played out.

These conflicts, however, usually exhaust themselves on derivative questions like (say) should Dante be included on a required reading list, when the main question, once again, should be: what are the required reading list and its representation of the one thing needful designed to accomplish? Among the values and goals customarily proposed or implicit are jumbled together all those that have appeared here, and over two centuries, as markers of liberal and civic education, beginning with the clash between Oxford and the *Edinburgh Review*: training of the mental faculties, as Oxford and Cambridge aimed to do with classics and mathematics—and perhaps diverting the radical or rapscallion instincts of the young; compensating for the professional and commercial demands of society that determine most students' careers; educating students to be like Newman's gentleman, compassionate, prudent, patient, forbearing, courteous, considerate, tolerant, never inflicting pain; introducing the young to the (sinful) world outside the university; offering them the best that has been thought and said; cultivating an aesthetic sense or a historical sense; teaching objectivity; providing the foundations of a common social bond; preparing individuals to assume civic responsibilities. Of these intertwining purposes, which are principally intended, which subordinate? And what means are addressed to which ends? Furthermore, how do we know when ends, however defined, have been met? Liberal education remains a belief system that survives not so much through institutional self-understanding as through continued acts of faith.

In the United States, which is unlike European nations in

this respect, these acts of faith rest most deeply on the sense of social obligation that has come naturally to a nation of immigrants (a sense of obligation not extended, until recently, to the nation's indigenous peoples). We expect "liberal education" to provide something more than compensation for the professional and commercial ways of the world—though we believe that a sense of social obligation corrects for limitations of the professional and commercial. We also expect something more from "great books" than aesthetic rewards—though we believe that aesthetic sensibilities contribute in their way to the fulfilling of civic responsibilities. And, whether we favor the multicultural curriculum or not, we argue our side of the case by referring to societal needs, to the claims of diversity or, alternatively, to the values of the melting pot. But the crucial fact, which is a crucial problem, is this: the tradition of "Western Civilization" arose out of ideas, practices, and attitudes so deeply ingrained as to have precluded serious inquiry into the relationship between social ends and curricular means, between civic and liberal education.

Only such inquiries, carefully thought out, could make sense of the question whether it is more important—that is, more useful—to read the *Inferno* than to read, say, Ralph Ellison's *Invisible Man*. The question has no meaning and no good answer unless it proceeds from an understanding of purpose: whether to require the reading of Dante or to require the reading of Ellison is by itself a preposterous dilemma. And posing one against the other in a sort of cultural showdown neglects larger issues that should be but seldom are addressed. If the end of responsible social participation is in fact at the heart of the matter, and if the study of texts, for whatever good reasons, is to be the means of achieving it, why are certain texts, of the highest relevance (one might suppose) and meeting at least some of the usual criteria, excluded from the start? Once again, the aggregation of practices sanctioned by custom, and incorporating the multiplicity of purposes embedded in the idea of liberal education, has made it next to impossible to think matters back to the beginning.

I have in mind the case of Stanford's "sacred" fifteen required texts. They included the Bible, Homer, Plato, Augustine, Dante, Luther, Darwin, Freud, and others—but no Franklin or Thoreau or Emerson. One response to this might follow Dana Munro's line of reasoning about medieval history, that the list provided an objective, because in a sense remote, ground of study; another response is that we need above all to know our European "heritage." But in fact the purposes of the list, beyond that of providing a shared body of material, are uncertain, especially so if its guiding motive is somehow to enforce a sense of social obligation. The cult of the sacred fifteen, for inherited reasons, introduced its initiates to a canon whose individual parts have little other than their canonicity in common and contribute only heterogeneously to an understanding of Western civilization or culture. But if some common reading list is in fact a desideratum, in the interests of social bonding, it should nonetheless be submitted to well thought out criteria of purposefulness. If no such criteria can be settled upon, or none empirically derived from such a list, that is the moment to ask whether canonicity itself provides an adequate basis for any requirement.

In the case of Edward Tylor's anthropological construction of "culture" or in the case of culture as it figures in "cultural studies," should either of them prevail decisively in the battle against Arnold's sweetness and light, criteria of purposefulness will be even more vital since both reject the canon of greatness. So long as cultural studies remain on the margins associated with a leftward-looking, working-class populism; so long, that is, as they define themselves in opposition to "Western Civilization" and thus end up as their adversary's mirror image, their criteria of purposefulness will be clear enough, as were the criteria when Stanford's Cathcart committee commented, "All freshman are either now or soon to be voters." But if cultural

studies were to take center stage, it could be predicted with
a fair degree of certainty that their ideological agenda would
blur over time, just as the ideology of Stanford's "Problems
of Citizenship" blurred over time and the course turned into
"Western Civilization." And if the liberal discipline of anthropology were to achieve the centrality that history and literature
have shared, it would confront from the outset the question, in
what should an introductory canon consist, assuming that the
end in sight were something other than professional initiation
in an academic discipline. In both cases, the risk would be that
of the canon's becoming, or being, unmanageable and hence of
re-creating, even within a requirement, a model carrying to its
(impossible) logical extreme Eliot's or Ezra Cornell's idea of the
ideal university as one in which everybody can study anything.

The problem of the "canon," about which literary people
argue parochially, is really a problem within a problem, namely,
the canon of learning as a whole. Or one might say that by
virtue of its convenience, the literary canon has become the sur-
rogate for the canon of culture in its Tylorian sense. If culture
is the sum total of habitual practices in a society, and if all the
habitual practices of society are thought of as equally worthy
of examination, what principles should govern the substantial
content of any requirement? Strong criteria are necessary to
ensure coherence. If we are to study the cultural practices of
different, infinitely divisible groups within the larger society,
whether defined by ethnicity, gender, class, or any other distinguishing marks, what should govern inclusions and exclusions
within any requirement? These are already burning questions.
And how are the claims of other cultural determinants—kin-
ship patterns, for example—to be judged against those of, say,
the "great books" considered as artifacts of a social structure?
The new standing of culture in its Tylorian sense challenges the
ingenuity of anyone who wants to preserve a commonalty of
learning so far as possible free from the heavy imprint of ideology: without a strong principle of selection, the logic of Tylorian culture runs strongly in the direction of an elective system

because so little or nothing can be excluded from categories of the relevant and the important. And if little or nothing is to be excluded, the situation again threatens to resemble that during and at the end of Eliot's 40-year presidency, when an absence at the center invited struggles of power and precedence. To the extent that political interests have taken over curricular debates, we can judge how close we may have come to this condition already.

"What to do?" is a provoking question, and not only because it finds no quick answers. It may also be taken to reflect the assumption that regularly, and not for the better, colors disputes about the curriculum, namely, that *everything* is always at stake. The assumption reflects, however unconsciously, Hutchins's belief that education ought to be independent of local constraints, that good education in a democracy will be equally good in an oligarchy, that good education in America does not (ideally) differ from that in any other country, and, by implication, that what is good for Chicago is equally good for Columbia, Michigan, California, Princeton, and Yale. On this view, urgent national interest rides on any local decision because it engages matters of universal significance; local considerations and conditions are therefore unworthy to be seriously examined. In a study of Hutchins's Chicago, William McNeill describes the mood during the early years of Hutchins's presidency: "Convinced of the universal importance of the issues so heatedly discussed . . . , members of the University of Chicago often seemed both provincial and smug. Many believed that they, and they alone, were wrestling with basic questions about education and the pursuit of truth." Though it was a heady time, though McNeill, then an undergraduate, delighted in it, and though he believes that Hutchins was right "in trying so hard to make the goals of higher education explicit," he sees at the distance of 50 years the consequences, in provinciality and smugness, of proposing universal remedies in the American context.[6]

This is a lesson to be taken to heart, especially now when

public attitudes—at least as it comes to education—run in favor of national rather than local solutions. Indeed the universities may not be the worst offenders. When Harvard's core curriculum came under criticism, James Q. Wilson, chairman of the task force that had recommended it, responded, "There is nothing most of us would like better than to be left alone in this enterprise—not because we have no use for criticism, but because we do not see Harvard as a model for what all colleges ought to be."[7] Yet this is perhaps a wishful, retrospective effort at disentanglement, not unlike the Redbook's about-face when it proclaimed itself as speaking for Harvard, not for American education at large.

The realities of the local do matter, a proposition that does not sit well with some critics of the educational system. We have risked losing sight of these realities altogether. It is just their value that E. D. Hirsch neglects in *Cultural Literacy* (1987), to the detriment of an argument that, though benignly intended, would have smug and provincializing results in practice. Hirsch's subtitle is *What Every American Needs to Know*, and no amount of demurral that the famous list appended to his text of "what literate Americans know" is descriptive, not prescriptive, can efface the sense that the list in all its arbitrariness represents what Hirsch believes every American really does *need* to know. Hirsch himself says, "My aim in this book is to contribute to making that information the possession of all Americans." If he were to prevail, every American would "know" the line, included in Hirsch's list, "There is no joy in Mudville." Among the most local of our cultural outposts, Mudville is not necessarily the worse for that. But why should "mighty Casey" be a household name equally in El Paso, Nome, Crown Heights, and Acoma Pueblo?[8]

As is sometimes said (by, for example, the committee that produced the Redbook) but less often reflected in moments of curricular conflict, American higher education has thrived in its heterogeneity. Not only are there public universities, private universities, liberal arts colleges, state colleges, and junior colleges, but within those groupings lie emphases and institutional habits of every sort. Real concessions to the regional and to the sheer differences of diversity would be an antidote to the provinciality of the universal reflected in Hutchins's Chicago or in Hirsch's list. Partly structural and partly regional, diversity should not be ignored by institutions in the pursuit of self-importance, and studies of education "at Stanford" or elsewhere neglect it at their peril. And when institutions do take their local differences into account—as in some instances they have had to do, for example at Mills College—such exigencies still need thoughtful translation at the level of the curriculum.

In the headlong rush to be the "best" (much as Charles Eliot would have welcomed it), American universities have not attended closely to whatever has made them what they are and therefore has influenced what they can become. As the product of what is by now a considerable history, American universities (when was the last one founded?) no longer offer a *tabula rasa* on which reformers may inscribe any characters they please. Studies of education "at ———" should take into account local circumstance, not at the expense of principle but with an eye to those for whom the curriculum is planned, to ingrained habits of the place, to whatever marks its difference from, as well as its similarity to, others of its kind. That should not, in theory, be difficult to do, if only because the selling of the institution in the student marketplace relies on claims of uniqueness. But when the curriculum is under consideration, different values typically apply.

The two universities I know best, Harvard and Stanford, differ as much from each other as California from Massachusetts. Of their differences, demographic and otherwise, some might be supposed *a priori* to bear on the curriculum but are seldom attended to. The two compete for many of the same students (Harvard annually wins the competition, at least numerically), but not on the basis of their curricula; instead each presents its

wares, in contrast with those of (say) the great institutes of technology, as standard liberal fare. Nothing (I concede) is likely
to change this strategy greatly, but local differences could be
factored in without a loss of catholicity and with an increased
potential for achieving the benign result that James Q. Wilson
pleaded for in response to critics of Harvard's "core": to be
left alone. More attention to the local could leave the universities better able, because more free, to do whatever job they are
trying to do.

A case in point: at Harvard, engineering is a minor presence;
at Stanford, something like one-fifth of all undergraduates take
a degree in engineering. At any one time, perhaps a hundred of
Stanford's undergraduate engineers major in the field that led
Irving Babbitt to fret about the prospect of degrees in a science
of plumbing. From Stanford's School of Engineering came the
most influential of the university's provosts, Frederick Terman,
previously dean of the School and before that chairman of Electrical Engineering. The importance of this School is a plain fact
of Stanford's life, though one regarded by some on the humanities faculty as unfortunate—and as the occasion for melancholy
zeal in spreading the liberal gospel. On the engineers' side, some
grumbling accompanies any new requirements because their
students' plates are already full to overflowing. What has not
been adequately considered is how the intellectual demography of the undergraduate population might affect educational
desiderata.

The counterargument, that what matters is not intellectual
demography but the ideal homogeneity represented by a Stanford degree, underestimates the possibility of crafting general
requirements that not only engage engineers in questions (at
present imperfectly conceived) of social responsibility but also
offer them a liberal education that is something more than a
type of cultural solace, while at the same time equipping students of literature or philosophy or history better to understand the cultural history and imperatives of engineering and

technology. This is not a matter, as C. P. Snow would have it, of explaining to humanists the second law of thermodynamics. Rather it is a matter, as much as in any "multicultural" situation, of cultural crossover and mutual comprehension.

The presence of Galileo's *Sidereus Nuncius* among Stanford's sacred fifteen represented an effort to incorporate within the rubric of "Western Culture" an understanding not just of science but of how science actually gets done. So did the presence of Stanford's program called "Values, Technology, Science, and Society" among the family of "Western Culture," but it was something of a poor cousin in that family, having to dig out the technological significance of Augustine's *Confessions*. Very much more might be tried. A founding text like Norbert Wiener's *Cybernetics* (1948; revised, 1961), a few sections of which require no familiarity with the language of mathematics, or his less technical *The Human Use of Human Beings* (1950) have as much claim to inclusion in the Western canon as Hobbes's *Leviathan*, Wollstonecraft's *Rights of Woman*, or anything of Freud's. What could be more compelling as a matter of human concern than Wiener's proposition, "We may be facing one of those limitations of nature in which highly specialized organs reach a level of declining efficiency and ultimately lead to the extinction of the species," or again, "The human brain may be as far along on its road to this destructive specialization as the great nose horns of the last of the titanotheres"?[9] Nor need fiction be left out. The masterpieces of modern technological fiction—William Gibson's *Neuromancer* (1984), in which he invented "cyberspace," or the stories of Philip K. Dick, for example—command an audience as passionate as that for any other "classic" of Western imaginative literature. That materials like these have not found their way into the standard curriculum is partly because engineers and scientists, not necessarily to their own advantage, make few demands on the canon. In Charles Eliot's kind of university "demands" do bear results, no matter how troublesome that may be to those in charge.

Lacking adequate criteria of purpose, we do not know how well our higher education works in practice or even exactly what working well would mean. We could do better on both counts.[10] The universities need not only to understand their own history better and how that history intersects with the larger history of the nation but also (once more) to understand what they have been trying individually and collectively to do—and then, as good sense may suggest, take steps needed to bring ends and means into closer alignment.

Finally, in the large social arena where educational questions come into play, more charitable habits of mind would not be a bad thing, either.

Appendix

'Citizenship in a Democratic World'

by Edgar Eugene Robinson

[As director of Stanford's "Problems of Citizenship," Robinson gave the opening and closing lectures of the course. For the year 1928–29, both survive in printed form. The opening lecture is reprinted here; the closing lecture was entitled "The Politics of Citizenship." I have not located the syllabus to which Robinson refers in the first paragraph of "Citizenship in a Democratic World," but the shape of the course is visible in a year-long schedule of lectures that was appended to his text. According to this schedule, the lectures in the first of three quarters were, first, "Citizenship in a Democratic World," then "Scientific Method and Attitude," "Evolution of Man," "Types of Human Behavior," "Early Development of Man," "Beginnings of Civilization," "Man's Co-operation with Nature," "Development of Social Science," "Sources of Information," and "Value and Use of Opinion." The lectures in the second quarter were "Intelligence in a Democracy," "The Citizen and the Vote," "Representative Government," "Political Parties," "Cost of Government," "Expenditures of Government," "The Railroad Problem," and "The Trust Problem."

"Citizenship in a Democratic World" (1928) is reprinted by permission of the Department of Special Collections, Stanford University Libraries (Stanford University Archives, SC 29A, Box 7, #208).

Those in the third quarter were "Liberty of the Citizen," "Minorities," "Limitations upon Classes," "Status of the Immigrant," "The Question of Race," "Co-operation in Industry," "The World Order," "American Participation," "Internationalism," and, to end the course, "The Politics of Citizenship." Transcripts of most of these lectures, and more than one printed version, also survive (Stanford University Archives, SC 29A, Box 7, #208). Readings appear to have been assigned from a "source-book," organized according to categories that Robinson identifies in his lecture: "Problems of Approach and Method," "Problems of Control and Support [of Government]," and "Problems of Liberty and Co-operation." Included were writings by Herbert Hoover, Walter Lippmann, James Bryce, Bertrand Russell, David Starr Jordan, and Robinson himself, among many others. Additional texts were available with periodicals and newspapers in the Citizenship Reading Room. A list of these texts (Stanford University Archives, SC 29A, Box 7, #200) survives for the year 1932–33. Included over three quarters were Boas's *The Mind of Primitive Man* and works by (for example) John Dewey, Herbert Hoover, John Maynard Keynes, Harold Laski, Walter Lippmann, Robert S. Lynd, Henri Poincaré, and John Herman Randall—adding up to more than 200 titles.

Robinson's opening lecture was a set piece. In *American Democracy in Time of Crisis* (Stanford, Calif.: Stanford University Press, 1934), he published four lectures he had given on various occasions, including his opening lecture for "Problems of Citizenship" in 1933–34, abridged and amended from the version of 1928. Principal changes were the excision of 1928's "young lady" (p. 140) who left the voting to the men of her family and the substitution of a final paragraph more appropriate to the hard times of 1933.

Two sections of the 1928 lecture (p. 134 and p. 137) illustrating attitudes that eventually converted "Problems of Citizenship" to "Western Civilization" are printed in italics. Best displaying the turn from civics to civilization are two sentences on page 134: "Thus it is that in seeking an alert, intelligent, and efficient citizenry we do not confine our attention to the structure and functions and theories of government. We are dealing first of all with man himself." These sentences survived intact in 1933, with the insertion of a single sentence between them, pointing to the prevalence of civics and related subjects in high schools: "Many of you have had much of this in earlier work" (*American Democracy in Time of Crisis*, pp. 53–54). The turn from civics to civilization and its history represents in part the failed dream of creating a social *science*. In *Current Problems in Citizenship* (New York: Macmillan, 1924), Harvard's William Bennett Munro, professor of "municipal government," announced with a hint of regret: "The real nature of a current problem is frequently related to its origin, and for this origin we must sometimes go a long way back. The social studies cannot be entirely dissociated from history; their relations are too intimate" (p. vii).]

To the Freshmen entering Stanford:

You have entered Stanford University as freshmen, and you are now enrolled in the course in Problems of Citizenship, a course of lectures, readings, and discussions which will continue throughout the year. A printed syllabus is in your hands.* You will attend one lecture each week on Tuesday at ten o'clock. Fifteen members of the faculty representing ten departments of the University are to give these lectures. Three times a week you will report to an instructor in Citizenship to whom you have been assigned, and under his direction and guidance you will carry on the work of the course. He will explain the details of this classwork, the methods in reading, and the nature of the topics to be prepared. Careful notes upon the lectures, systematic reading in the books listed on the syllabus, and an active participation in the discussions in class are all essential to satisfactory progress in this work.

As you read widely in the printed materials available to you and listen to lectures on the various subjects included, it is to be

---

*"Syllabus of Lectures and Readings" and "Outline of Class Work for Sections," Stanford University Press.

expected that you will find opportunity to correlate much of the knowledge that you have acquired in your preparatory schooling, and that gradually you will not only improve upon your methods of study and thought, but that you will also begin to formulate certain principles by which you intend to test conclusions and programs that are brought to your attention. It will presently become clear what is meant by the statement that in the study of the problems of citizenship we are engaged in a right ordering of our several loyalties.

As you begin this year to lay the foundations for work in your special field of interest, built as they are upon still earlier foundations, so too you are called upon to build carefully and to prepare thoughtfully for your work as a citizen. For citizenship, as Thomas Arnold pointed out long ago, is the second calling of every man and woman. You will observe as we go forward that our constant endeavor will be to relate what we do and say to the facts of the world from which you came and in which all of you will live, and to correlate the various aspects of the modern scene, so that it will appear that citizenship is not a thing apart, something to be thought of only occasionally or left to the energies of a minority of our people, but that its proper understanding is at the very root of our daily life. It is a personal matter, just as all education is a matter for the individual. We begin our labor this year with an old conviction, so sorely tried in the speed and impersonality of the present day, that there is a possibility of insisting upon standards of personal conduct, in public affairs as in private life, powerful enough to bring into existence, and to continue in existence, an honest, effective, and purposeful world.

Some of you may be familiar with the fact that when Senator and Mrs. Stanford prepared the Founding Grant of this University they declared that its object was "to qualify its students for personal success and direct usefulness in life, and its purposes to promote the general welfare by exercising an influence on behalf of humanity and civilization, teaching the blessings of

liberty regulated by law, and inculcating love and reverence for
the great principles of government as derived from the inalien-
able right of man to life, liberty, and the pursuit of happiness."
Nearly twenty years later, in 1902, Mrs. Stanford, the surviving founder, in a supplementary decree declared: "The moving
spirit of the founders . . . was love of humanity and desire to
render the greatest possible service to mankind. . . . The public at large and not alone the comparatively few students who
attend the University are the chief and ultimate beneficiaries of
this foundation. While the instruction offered must be such as
will qualify the students for personal success and direct usefulness in life, they should understand that it is offered in the hope
and trust that they will become thereby of greater service to the
public."

Senator Stanford was an outstanding figure in the public life
of California and of the nation for many years. He gave of his
time, his energy, and his ability to public affairs. So too have
hundreds of the graduates of the University. The presidents of
this University have done distinguished work in the public service, as have many of the faculty. Measured by a leadership in
matters of local, state, national, or international importance,
this University has amply justified the hopes of its founders.
But it is doubtful whether such leadership was so much in their
minds as was the creation of an informed body of citizens who,
as members of the community and voters in elections, should
bring to the problems of politics an alert intelligence, a lively
sense of reality, and standards by which to judge leaders and
measures. We may assume that they had in mind a preparation for citizenship as a problem in education, rather than the
development of a technique in Political Science, Economics,
or Law.

We may judge that this was the approach of the faculty of
Stanford University some seven years ago when a committee,
in reporting upon certain changes in curriculum, including a
required course in citizenship, said: "Generally speaking, all

freshmen are either now or soon to be voters. Does not the University owe them a duty as such? If our tritest sayings are true these freshmen are destined to become leaders in their respective communities. They are forming the political and economic and social ideas that will characterize that leadership. And they are forming them now while the air is full of strange doctrines and without waiting for a critical and scholarly insight. Can the University not render a substantial social service by providing a sound basis of elementary scientific facts and principles by which the validity of these doctrines may be tested?"

When these words were written most of you, members of this class of 1932, were less than twelve years old. You are right in expecting that in the intervening years there has been some thinking, as well as other forms of activity, touching upon this work at Stanford. *The situation of 1928 is unlike that of 1920; most of all in the shift of interest to a consideration of man's relation to his environment, his capacity to feel and to think, his powers of discrimination, his dependence upon public opinion, his intelligence; altogether his capacities as a thinking man. Thus it is that in seeking an alert, intelligent, and efficient citizenry we do not confine our attention to the structure and functions and theories of government. We are dealing first of all with man himself.* This will lead some of you to say that it is abstract; and some may echo the cry of the student who said, "Give me something definite, even though it isn't true." But patience will presently be rewarded with a sure grasp of a method of procedure. At Stanford as freshmen you are to devote about a fourth of the time of your first year to this work. Despite the reasons which have just been given, it has appeared to many that this was a great deal of time to spend on a subject not directly related to preparation for a business or a profession. It has been seriously maintained by parents and students, as well as by some members of the faculty, that there is no time for such "extras" now that the student has entered college. This is an old cry with which educators have long been familiar. Said an eager father to James A. Garfield, then president of Hiram College, "My boy hasn't any time for all these studies. Get him through quickly." "Well," replied Garfield, "it all depends upon what you want. When God wants to make an oak He takes a hundred years, but He takes only two months to make a squash." We must begin to realize that there is a difference between the freedom to choose an objective and the ability to choose the proper way to reach that objective.

The desire to hurry over these college years is not so prevalent as it once was. Indeed the emphasis in recent years has been upon an enlargement and improvement of the groundwork taken in the first two years of the college course. There is an agreement that every university has the means of giving all of its students certain elementary principles, both in social and natural sciences, and that it has a duty to do so. When Stanford first undertook to do this six years ago it was a pioneer. At Dartmouth College and at Columbia University experiments of a similar order were going forward, but little elsewhere. Three years ago there were a dozen institutions giving serious attention to the problem. In a recent compilation it is reported that nearly sixty institutions will give work of this general character to freshmen this year. The time may come when Stanford will provide not only courses in the study of public affairs, but a definite program leading to the profession of politics, as men now prepare for Law, Engineering, Medicine, and Education. Johns Hopkins and Syracuse have made beginnings in this direction. But for the present we are concerned with the transformation that has come over introductory courses. College education is always in a process of transformation. But it is now apparent that the changes of recent years have created conditions which must lead to fundamental educational changes in years to come. We are on the threshold of a great opportunity.

You are entering college at a time when there is growing acceptance of the view that in the social sciences there should be analysis and criticism not alone by the experts in those fields but by those who, as educated men and women, are to have an adequate comprehension and a trustworthy technique in handling the affairs of government and country. Such a view asks that men turn away from traditional ways of thinking and acting when they are shown to be irrational, and undertake to establish new procedures based upon facts scientifically established. It is not enough just to point out past mistakes and present fallacies. "Reason must take the field to criticize our institutions," as Meiklejohn has said.

Just now at Stanford this course is prescribed for all students, because it is designed to prepare all to do what they can in community effort. It is impossible to think accurately, vote intelligently, participate productively in public affairs without a preparation in the make-up of society. To do this effectively, it is necessary to construct a considerable background. We must be sure we know what American objectives are and have been. We must be sure we have a reliable method of procedure. In a university many departments are concerned with public affairs, but certain departments are more directly interested than others. In particular is it the work of the social sciences, the departments of economics, political science, sociology, philosophy, and history. From these departments and from others will come the men who are to develop the problems of citizenship in the lectures given during the year.

You will find that the outline of work for the sections presents six problems: Approach, Method, Control, Support, Liberty, and Co-operation; and we are now ready to consider the point of view which we shall maintain in considering these problems. We shall insist upon no final solutions, contenting ourselves with presenting the essentials of each problem, their place in the modern scene, and the principles involved in various programs of solution. We shall bear in mind constantly that, as Herbert Croly has said, "the subject-matter of social science is the activities of human beings who are above everything else themselves."

Now a comprehensive grasp of the problems of citizenship

necessitates first of all a consideration of the preparation of the thoughtful members of the human race for taking up the task of furnishing solutions for the problems which have arisen. In particular is it necessary to consider the environments, physical, historical, and mental, in which the citizen finds himself. "The student of citizenship," wrote Nathaniel Shaler years ago, "whether as a youth he is trying to understand his own place in the world, or as an adult man he is endeavoring to see into the problems of the society he has to help, does best to begin his inquiry by studying certain lessons which modern science has taught us concerning the origin and nature of man." Such an approach involves consideration of the evolution of man and of the scientific method and scientific attitude in the study of his attempts to better himself.

We shall consider the "mental content" which must anticipate any discussion of habit and of the place of instinct. Emotion and reflection are considered in order to give a more complete picture of the human being as far as we shall consider him here. Of course the place of intelligence will be given definite emphasis, not only in the way of testing its manifestations, but also in its influence upon the functioning of democracy. Throughout these early weeks the scientific attitude as a point of view will be constantly kept in mind, and more and more attention given to the scientific method as offering a possible solution in the way of action as well as of thought in the field of social relationships.

All this would appear to turn your attention to an investigation of the sources of information, not only the information available in the present day, but sources from which all that you have in mind has been drawn. Then follows naturally the discussion of the formation of public opinion and a consideration of the search for truth and its recognition. In this work you will have occasion to use the special reading room set aside for the class in Citizenship. Here you will find the current periodicals and six of the more important daily papers.

We next take up the problem of control of government, which includes a consideration of political democracy. All subjects here considered will be approached as illustrating or defining the problem of the individual in attaining his objectives, exercising his privileges, and performing his duties. During this period, forms of government and principles of political science are to be presented only as they aid in the explanation of the problem of control.

Government must be supported. This leads directly to the problem of taxation from the point of view of the citizen, and then to methods of taxation. These cannot be dealt with adequately except as attention is given to the role of the government in the control of currency and banking, and this may properly introduce an adequate setting for consideration of the protective feature in tariff-making. The social burdens of government will be considered, including the cost of social-service activities.

Somewhat apart from government has grown up the structure of society in meeting the problem of subsistence. The institution of private property and the modern economic system bear a conditioning relation to the situation of the citizen as he is seeking his livelihood and attempting to keep his place as a worker, as an employer, or perhaps not clearly as either one. Because of the insistence of the case, he cannot avoid contact with the need of considering the advantages of bargaining in groups, the strength of government regulation, the role of the government in the way of protection. Finally there will be consideration of the question of public ownership and operation. The economic needs of the individual man are a primary factor in his consideration of government.

Having given the citizen his place in relation to the control of property, either the structure of government or the manifold forms of private ownership, attention will be directed to the problems involving persons. This should begin with a view of the problems growing out of the claims of personal liberty, particularly in America. We turn then to political liberty and the consideration of liberalism and of revolution.

Continuing the emphasis upon persons, we examine the conflict of peoples, races, and classes. The conflict between men and women, being essentially personal, belongs here, as do the questions of labor. We consider the proposals for radical reform. Finally, as a problem, not primarily of property interest (although present), nor of government method (although important), we have the co-operation of peoples, leading to the citizen's relation to the question of war and to the movements for the development of internationalism and for the maintenance of the peace of the world.

We shall see then that from this point of view, the co-operation of the people of the world (which lies within the action of its citizens) grows out of a better understanding (in the way of adjustment) of the inevitability of the mixture of peoples, races, and classes, and of the importance of the problem of individual liberty. These in turn are given their vital place in the emotional life, as well as in the thoughtful life of man, in that individual livelihood is the basis of the industrial problem, and that individuals in the mass support the government in whatever it does, and that co-operation makes for a degree of control of the government. All this follows upon an appreciation that action, whether of the individual or of the group, draws upon sources of information and, again, that information depends not only upon existent sources, but in large measure upon the education of the individual and the earlier growth and development of the society in which he is now living. And to begin with, there must be the conception of the evolutionary character of society and the relation of action and thought of individuals to the well-being of the whole. This has given direction to the factors outlined in these problems. Throughout, social, economic, and political ideas will take precedence over principles, institutions, programs, theories, and most of all, solutions.

This conception of the study of Citizenship is then not that of an endeavor to support a faith nor to inculcate a dogma. It is intended to increase reliance upon reason, and to develop the critical faculties at the same time that it creates or leads to the desire to function actively and continuously in social relationships. It is an outgrowth of a conviction that independent, critical thought has a chance as against both Fascism and Communism. Dogmatic teaching of the field of citizenship has been productive of harm to society in that it has tended to close the channels of discussion and to curb individual initiative. There is little hope for the development of what Graham Wallas has termed "The Great Society" except through the progressive development of the power of thought and of the inclination toward co-operation among an increasing number of educated persons. And this is a convenient point to stress the fact that in your answers, oral and written, in this work you will not be in the position of a student who some years ago entered an institution of higher education in the East and was asked to take an examination. In this examination he answered one of the questions as best he could, but it did not please the examiner, and he was summoned to appear before the president. "Young man," said he, "in this institution you are not expected to think things out. You are to take what is given to you and write down what you are taught."

We are prepared now to consider the case of the reluctant student; that is, reluctant as far as such a course of study is concerned. We may distinguish two types. There is the one who wishes to place the burden on someone else, and frankly says so. A young lady registering at Stanford some years ago was advised to take a certain course because, said her adviser, it will give you the facts of American government and aid you in making your decisions at election time. "But," said she, in mock horror, "I won't think of voting. I leave that to my father and brother." There is a second type, no less familiar but not quite so frank. Such a one is too busy in college and afterward for public affairs, immersed as he is in his own affairs. He goes about his business, selling automobiles or bonds, writing stories, or building bridges, without an hour for thought of the society about him, the social structure that has made possible his present life, and which will support and protect him in all the years to come. He does not actually wish the task upon someone else; he merely assumes that it will be done somehow. Why worry about it? Of this type Wells is writing when in *Meanwhile* he says, "What he wants is to be let alone. Why not leave him alone?" Of course that is one course of action. Cease to urge upon the people that they participate in election and that they prepare to do so. Permit the business of government to fall into the hands of a few interested persons and limit or abolish the whole educational process for preparing bodies of people to understand public affairs. Of course that has been done, and may be done again. But not in a democracy.

Men have grown so dependent upon one another in the last fifty years that it is becoming increasingly less likely that any great number of educated men and women will adopt this lazy attitude toward democracy. Courses like this one and movements elsewhere throughout the country to draw attention to public affairs are symptomatic of the growth of the belief that it is dangerous to let things drift. We found that particularly true at the time when the United States entered the war. We were not only physically unprepared for war but also mentally unprepared for the implications of that war. As long as man lived in comparative isolation it made little difference to him what happened in adjacent, and certainly in distant, areas; but with the increase in the means of communication that have bound the world in the last thirty-five years, the actual world is growing smaller and smaller, and we are not free to ignore what takes place in the next state or the next nation, or anywhere in the world.

When we speak of an educated man we mean educated not only in the sense of the possession of facts, but the ability to use them, or in a phrase of David Starr Jordan's "to arrange facts so they mean something." The educated man listens and reads, and then he does what the mass of men do not yet do, he reasons about it. The educated classes in England and in Scotland are excellent examples of this, and it is probable that the success of the English in government, in executive efficiency, popular control, and individual freedom, may be traced to the fact that many educated Englishmen do more than listen and read: they proceed to the point of thought and reason in advance of action. Take, for example, an impending coal strike in America. The man we are considering cannot be content to take the statements of operators or miners. Much less would he be content to take only one of these. He must get a various information and he must get it from many sources. He must know something of costs of transportation, of methods of mining, of living conditions of the workers, of the state of the financial market, if he is to get at a contribution in the public interest. It is hard in the midst of a world in which self-interest and hurry are dominant notes to get at the facts or to get the time to use those facts. It is apparent that only a few educated men and women can be counted upon to do it.

The hope of democracy from the point of view of men and women of education lies in the use and development of the instrumentalities that they find ready for use. The road to a more and more satisfactory state of affairs lies in perfecting the instrumentalities which our forefathers have left to us. This is another way of saying that violent revolution does not pay. The cost outreaches the advantages and generations pay the cost. War is the most ghastly example of how not to conduct society. Man has simply failed to use his mind.

An instrumentality which interests us is the ballot box. In the United States, unlike some other nations that might be named, we have come to look upon ballots as instruments more effective than bullets for the satisfaction of the interests of our citizens. But the general acceptance of the ballot does not carry with it the easy acceptance of all the results that come from the ballot box. The existence of trial by ballot provides for another ballot. A system of government which provides for voting should never close the door. There are men and women in California and elsewhere who tell you that there are some public questions that are settled. The moment you claim that a matter of public interest is settled finally you are virtually denying the reason for the existence of a system of balloting and one of the fundamentals of democracy. If you don't want democracy you may argue that way, but democracy asks that the doors of discussion be kept open. An English conservative with whom I was talking two years ago spent a great deal of wrath upon what he termed endless discussion, saying, "What we have in England is too much discussion. . . . If these idiots would only stop trying to change things. . . . We have got too much education." And I might have reminded him of an Englishman, Sir William Berkeley, who came out to Virginia three hundred years ago, and who wrote back to his King, "I thank God there are no free schools, nor printing, and I hope we shall not have, these hundred years; for learning has brought disobedience, and heresy, and sects into the world, and printing has divulged them, and libels against the best of government. God keep us from both." In America, as it developed into a nation, there was always a reminder of the price of democracy. As Dr. Hadley succinctly says: "A liberal education is an education for liberty—the kind of education needed by a free man."

Something ought to be said here about the relation of this course to other courses, because there ought to be no misunderstanding at the outset. It is necessarily and intentionally introductory. The subject-matter you will find in the section of the syllabus given over to classwork. This subject-matter presents some of the elements and fundamentals of the social sciences, but it does not attempt to provide an introduction to any one of them. This course is introductory to all your college work because it provides an introduction in methods of study and discussion. Furthermore, it aims to place you in more intimate touch with what is often neglected in the university, to put you in touch with the intellectual currents outside the university, with educated men and women who write for our great newspapers and magazines; also, to call your attention to the growth of your mind. Said the late Charles W. Eliot of Harvard, addressing a group of freshmen: "You ought to obtain here the trained capacity for mental labor, rapid, intense, and sustained. That is the great thing to get in college long before the professional school is entered. Get it now. Get it in the years of college life. It is the main achievement of college life to win this mental force, this capacity for keen observation, just inference, and sustained thought, for everything that we mean by the reasoning power of man." Observe that in the modern day there is one thing that ought to distinguish leaders in a democracy and that is the use of their minds. Thus we reject both the authoritarian and the dogmatic methods in education.

You will hear a great deal in the days to come, not in this course, but in your life at Stanford, about loyalty to Stanford. In the past thirty years in every part of the world, Stanford men and women have done fine things, and Stanford has a fine heritage of public service. It is a precious heritage and you may have your part. Here is your chance to lay the foundation for it in the use of the mind. The career of an educated man or woman—it is yours, if you will only claim it, and if you do you will help fulfill the desire of the founders of the University to further the public service in the foundation of a university. President Wilbur said, a year ago, upon returning from the meeting of the Institute of Pacific Relations at Honolulu, "If men of good spirit and good will can get together on a common basis of scientific interest and a desire to study out the facts, the nations of the world can work out their problems through their citizens." In this spirit I hope you will begin your work.*

---

*In the published version of Robinson's 1933 lecture, the final paragraph runs as follows: "In the present hour you are on the threshold of your opportunity. No group has a greater call to thought and to service. For as has been said, 'A generation . . . like our own, whose feet lie so near the abyss, has no right to optimism about the future; the fact that it knows the way is no proof that it will choose the way.'" (*American Democracy in Time of Crisis*, p. 62.)

Reference Matter

Notes

I

1. Eliot, "What Is a Liberal Education?" p. 120.
2. Bloom, p. 346; Searle, p. 34; Baldick, p. 1; Bell, p. 181.
3. Eliot, "What Is a Liberal Education?" p. 120.
4. Menand, p. 55.
5. For an overview of education and the ideal of citizenship in the United States, see Rothblatt, "Modern Citizenship."
6. Pelikan, p. 193.

II

1. Morison, pp. 344–45.
2. On the contest between science and religion and the origins of the American university, see Reuben.
3. Wertenbaker, p. 307.
4. Eliot, "Liberty in Education," p. 125.
5. *Ibid.*, pp. 147, 148. On universities and the urban setting, see Bender, ed.
6. Eliot, "Liberty in Education," pp. 125, 126.
7. *Ibid.*, p. 127.
8. *Ibid.*
9. Veysey, p. 82; Jordan, 1: 114; James, 1: 349, 331; Hawkins, p. 143.
10. Hawkins, p. 289; A. Smith, 2: 363. I am grateful to George Dekker for the reference to Smith.
11. Eliot, "Liberty in Education," p. 145.
12. Weber, p. 25.
13. Eliot, "Liberty in Education," p. 137.

14. On Eliot and "race," see Hawkins, pp. 180–84, 190–93. On Darwin and "nativism," see Higham, pp. 135–36.

15. McCosh, p. 4.

16. Eliot, "Liberty in Education," pp. 144, 140, 141.

17. McCosh, pp. 3–4, 11.   18. *Ibid.*, pp. 10, 11.

19. Bell, pp. 187–88.   20. McCosh, p. 11.

21. *Ibid.*, p. 16.   22. Sumner, p. 853.

23. McCosh, p. 29.

24. Cf. Rothblatt, *The Idea of the Idea of a University*, pp. 7, 9: "If Newman loved what he wanted Oxford to stand for, he also disliked very passionately a new and rival conception of a university that had arisen in the metropolis in the late 1820s, the University of London. We must bear this situation in mind as we proceed to understand just what the Cardinal meant when he said that a university—and he meant all universities—contained, that is, *should* contain, an idea. . . . The idea of a university is that it must ultimately produce whole people."

III

1. Dewey, 2: 499.

2. Playfair, pp. 282, 283; Knight, p. 429; S. Smith, pp. 48, 51.

3. On the history of "liberal education," see B. A. Kimball, and Rothblatt, *Tradition and Change*; also Slee, *Learning and a Liberal Education* and "The Oxford Idea of a Liberal Education," and Garland. For a consideration of liberal education that is "not a treatise, a study, or a history" but "an attempt to rediscover and redefine a persistent problem" (p. vii), see Wegener.

4. Rothblatt, *Tradition and Change*, pp. 119–22, 122. Rothblatt amplifies his argument in "The Student Sub-culture." The examination statute of 1800 is quoted in Ward, p. 13.

5. Copleston, *Advice*, pp. 74–75.

6. Copleston, *A Reply*, p. 149.

7. Cockburn, p. 22.

8. Knight, Playfair, and Smith, p. 182.

9. Copleston, *A Reply*, p. 150.

10. Edgeworth, p. 156; Copleston, *A Reply*, pp. 110, 111. Edgeworth's doubts about the value of a classical education extended even to the case of statesmen: "Here it must again be lamented that so much more time than is necessary is devoted to Latin and Greek" (p. 416).

11. Copleston, *A Reply*, pp. 111, 112.

12. Hamilton, p. 401.

13. Knight, Playfair, and Smith, p. 187.

14. Hamilton, pp. 784; 785; 786–87n. On the *Edinburgh Review* and the controversy with Oxford, see Engel, pp. 309–14.

15. Lyell, 1: 261.   16. *Ibid.*, pp. 268, 269, 270.

17. *Ibid.*, pp. 289, 290.   18. *Ibid.*, pp. 290–91.

19. Tyack, pp. 90–128.   20. Hawkins, p. 29.

21. Lyell, 1: 298, 299, 302, 306, 307.

22. Whewell, *Of a Liberal Education*, p. 117; Lyell, 1: 243; Whewell, *Of a Liberal Education*, p. 121. A small skirmish in the early nineteenth century's battle of the books had erupted when the *Edinburgh Review* published its notice of Whewell's *Thoughts on the Study of Mathematics* (1835); in the second edition (1836), Whewell included a brief response in the form of a letter to Macvey Napier, editor of the *Review*.

IV

1. Adamson, p. 17.

2. Ker, pp. 18–19; Newman, pp. 138–39.

3. Arnold, p. 107.

4. Ker, p. 383.

5. R. Kimball, pp. 39, 68. Johnson's words are also quoted in Bromwich, p. 100. According to Bromwich, who draws on a *New Republic* article of April 10, 1989—apparently the first citation of Johnson's statement, Johnson said that faculty are supposed to be creating not a better world but a better "community."

6. Newman, pp. 110, 111.   7. *Ibid.*, p. 179.

8. *Ibid.*, pp. 195, 138, 197.   9. *Ibid.*, pp. 197–98.

10. Quoted in DeLaura, p. 6.   11. Quoted in Raleigh, p. 78.

12. Raleigh, p. 87.   13. Arnold, pp. 241, 244–45.

14. Bishop, p. 74.

15. The second chapter of *Culture and Anarchy* is called "Doing as One Likes."

16. Arnold, pp. 238, 165, 243.

17. McBride, p. 60.

18. Arnold, pp. 164, 244, 223, 526.

V

1. Quoted in Solomon, p. 176.   2. Howe, pp. 92, 93.

3. *Ibid.*, p. 93.   4. *Ibid.*, p. 200; Wendell, p. 15.

5. W. Wilson, "The Spirit of Learning," p. 3.

6. Howe, p. 201; Wendell, p. 18; Howe, pp. 202, 203. In writing to his friend James Ford Rhodes on July 3, 1909, Wendell misremembered, made still more obscure, and even mutilated as follows the lines I cited above from the printed version of "De Praeside Magnifico": "As Edwards, holding Calvin's precepts true, / Preached them to practice, made them live anew, / So Eliot now arrests our happier state, / Edwards of Channing—each securely great" (Howe, p. 201). If "arrests" is not Howe's editorial error, then Wendell seems to have let more of his true feelings slip into this twisted version of his own lines. Channing does not figure in Hawkins, the nearest thing we have to an intellectual biography of Eliot, except in a mention of Wendell's ode. Probably Wendell remembers especially the selection of Channing's sermons edited by the latter's nephew William Henry Channing, and published in 1873 as *The Perfect Life*.

7. E.g.: "There seems no adequate reason why Latin and Greek should be regarded as a sort of linguistic Siamese twins, which nature has joined together, and which would wither if separated" (Sidgwick, p. 84).

8. Adams, p. 113.

9. *Ibid.*, pp. 130, 113, 115, 134.

10. *Ibid.*, pp. 119, 120.

11. *Ibid.*, pp. 132, 120, 124.

12. Sutton, 2: 590.

13. Haskins, 1: 149.

14. Allardyce, p. 695.

15. Both articles are reprinted (in part) in Graff and Warner, eds.

16. Hunt, p. 118.

17. On the ambiguousness of meaning in the concept of the humanities, see Rothblatt, "A Long Apocrypha." The process by which the current tripartite division of knowledge—humanities, social sciences, natural sciences—became conventional has not that I know been traced.

18. Tate, p. 132.

19. Babbitt, *Literature and the American College*, pp. 70, 96, 95, 128.

20. *Ibid.*, pp. 110, 83.

21. *Ibid.*, pp. 181, 180, 179.

22. *Ibid.*, p. 183.

23. Winters, p. 332; Cowley, pp. 84, 83.

24. E. Wilson, pp. 39, 39–40.

25. Winters, p. 333.

26. W. Wilson, "Mere Literature," p. 26.

27. Eliot, ed., *The Harvard Classics* 50: 10, 17, 70.

28. *Ibid.*, pp. 18, 11.

VI

1. Haskins, 1: 157, 154.
2. Higham, pp. 212–13.
3. On the influence of the war on literary criticism and scholarship in England, see Baldick, pp. 86–108.
4. Buchler, p. 54.
5. Haskins, 1: 171.
6. Solomon, pp. 94, 95, 61.
7. See A. B. Hart, Morse, Clark, and MacKibbin. Hart lists a series of 27 questions debated during the academic year 1887–88 in "Oral Discussion of Topics in Political Economy and History," a course in public speaking. The first was "Should immigration into the United States be restricted?" (p. 632).
8. "A National Reform League," p. 2; "Waite, Henry Randall," p. 318.
9. Higham, p. 46; Waite, ed., "The Civic Outlook," p. 324.
10. Waite, ed., "The Civic Outlook," pp. 211, 217; Goodale, pp. 367, 368; and Debs, e. g., p. 412: "The cry of 'anarchist' has about had its day."
11. Waite, "Civics," pp. 202–3; Paine, p. 320. For an early instance of "Civics" on the educational agenda, see Crehore. For a survey of new curricular requirements in universities after the war, see "Initiatory Courses for Freshmen." This report, by a committee of the American Association of University Professors, expresses a preference for freshman courses in "Thinking" and in "the Nature of the World and of Man" over those that emphasize citizenship (p. 34).
12. In Guitteau, p. xi.
13. *Annual Report of the President of Stanford University*, p. 18.
14. Quoted in Hofstadter and Smith, eds., 2: 904–5.
15. Randall, pp. 9, 10.
16. *Annual Report of the President of Stanford University*, p. 18.
17. Buchler, pp. 113–24.
18. Erskine, "Magic and Wonder in Literature," p. 167; Babbitt, *Rousseau and Romanticism*, p. 76.
19. Farrar, Preface, in *Great Books*, pp. 5, 8, 13.
20. Quoted in Buchler, p. 51.
21. Eliot, "What Is a Liberal Education?" p. 98.
22. Woodberry, *Great Writers*, p. 215.
23. Erskine, *The Delight of Great Books*, p. 29.
24. Suksdorf, pp. 8, 374. On the history of American racist thought,

see Gossett, especially, in connection with issues relevant here, pp. 123–43 and 287–369. Gossett does not make the connection between racism and "great books," though he devotes some space to Barrett Wendell. The egregious Suksdorf, a small fish in the big pond of racist thought, does not figure in Gossett's narrative. See Court on the racial consciousness associated with the emergence of English literary study—whose champions included F. D. Maurice at King's College, London, in the 1840s, and, after him, Arnold.

25. Woodberry, *The Torch*, pp. 7, 6, 12, 114.
26. Erskine, *The Influence of Women and Its Cure*, pp. 17, 20, 128.
27. Erskine, *The Delight of Great Books*, pp. 164, 166.
28. Hutchins, *The Higher Learning in America*, pp. 1, 105.
29. Hutchins, *The Great Conversation*, p. 1.
30. Ashmore, p. 260.
31. Hutchins, *The Great Conversation*, p. 2.
32. Bloom, p. 344. For a corrective to prevailing belief that Hutchins single-handedly organized the Chicago curriculum around "the powers and pleasures of the Great Books," see Donald N. Levine's Preface to *The Idea and Practice of General Education*, pp. v–vi.

VII

1. Gideonse, pp. 25, 28, 27, 28.
2. Quoted in Ashmore, p. 172.
3. Buck, p. 34.
4. *General Education in a Free Society*, p. 37.
5. *Ibid.*, p. 58.
6. Bell, p. 43.
7. *General Education in a Free Society*, pp. 205, 213–14.
8. *Ibid.*, pp. 207, 215, 216, 217.
9. *Ibid.*, pp. 3–4, 177, 183.
10. Rand, pp. 8, 16. By permission of The Harvard University Archives.
11. *General Education in a Free Society*, p. 183.
12. Morison, pp. 133–34.
13. *Harvard: 1956*, pp. 18, 22. The student authors of this issue of *i.e.* were Leo Raditsa; John A. Pope, Jr.; Angus Fletcher; and Peter Davis.
14. *Ibid.*, pp. 9, 12.
15. *The Study of Education at Stanford* 1: 3; 2: 10.
16. Arnold, p. 117.
17. *The Study of Education at Stanford* 2: 24; 1: 14.

18. *Ibid.* 2: 17, 16.

19. Allardyce, pp. 696, 725. Cf. Lougee, p. 726: "Professor Allardyce's diagnosis is incomplete because . . . outdated."

20. Allardyce, p. 725.

VIII

1. Barry Katz to W. B. Carnochan, May 26, 1992.

2. Tylor, 1: 1; and see Stocking. For a thoughtful account of "culture" as a vexed, unstable, historically conditioned concept—"a wavering, self-contradicting thing" (p. 20)—see Herbert.

3. Tylor, 1: 29, 31.   4. Stocking, p. 87.

5. Morgan, p. 514.   6. Boas, pp. 225, 253.

7. I make the assumption that the index in Miner, ed., is reliable.

8. Sapir, pp. 308, 314–15. I am grateful to Bernard Siegel for this reference.

9. Redfield, p. 145.

10. Bidney, "The Concept of Value," pp. 688, 689.

11. Bidney, *Theoretical Anthropology*, pp. 416, 432. On Bidney's influence, see Grindal and Warren, eds. On the "objectivity question" in general, see Novick, especially, in connection with anthropology, pp. 144–45, 284–86, 548–55.

12. Bidney, "The Concept of Value," p. 688.

13. Benedict, p. 7.

14. Johnson, p. 152.

15. Quoted (from Williams's *The Long Revolution* [1962]) in Johnson, p. 172.

16. Darcy, p. 15.

17. Geertz, p. 165.

18. "New CIV Courses in the Works," p. 1.

IX

1. Veblen, p. 34.

2. Buchler, pp. 196–97.

3. Wegener, p. 90.

4. Huxley, pp. 81, 80. I am grateful to Kenneth Fields for this reference.

5. Quoted in Keller, p. 69.   6. McNeill, p. viii.

7. Quoted in Keller, p. 146.   8. Hirsch, pp. xiv; 208.

9. Wiener, *Cybernetics*, p. 154. I am grateful to N. Katherine Hayles

for guidance in an area where she knows a great deal and I very little.

10. Harvard's "Assessment Seminars," initiated by President Derek Bok, are a recent serious effort to study successes and failures of the curriculum. Yet the method of in-depth interviews with students yields a sophisticated opinion survey; it does not address basic questions of purpose, nor could any such effort at "assessment." See Light.

Works Cited

Adams, Charles Francis. "Some Modern College Tendencies." In *Three Phi Beta Kappa Addresses*, pp. 99–147. Boston: Houghton Mifflin, 1907.

Adamson, John William. *English Education, 1789–1902.* Cambridge, Eng.: Cambridge University Press, 1930.

Allardyce, Gilbert. "The Rise and Fall of the Western Civilization Course." *American Historical Review* 87 (June 1982): 695–725.

Annual Report of the President of Stanford University for the Twenty-Ninth Academic Year Ending August 31, 1920. Stanford University, Calif.: Published by the University, 1920.

Arnold, Matthew. *Culture and Anarchy, with Friendship's Garland and Some Literary Essays.* In *The Complete Prose Works of Matthew Arnold*, vol. 5, ed. R. H. Super. Ann Arbor: University of Michigan Press, 1965.

Ashmore, Harry S. *Unseasonable Truths: The Life of Robert Maynard Hutchins.* Boston: Little, Brown, 1989.

Babbitt, Irving. *Literature and the American College: Essays in Defense of the Humanities*, intro. Russell Kirk. Washington, D.C.: National Humanities Institute, 1986 [1908].

———. *Rousseau and Romanticism.* New York: Meridian Books, 1955 [1919].

Baldick, Chris. *The Social Mission of English Criticism, 1848–1932.* Oxford: Clarendon Press, 1983.

Becker, Carl L. *The Heavenly City of the Eighteenth-Century Philosophers.* New Haven, Conn.: Yale University Press, 1932.

Bell, Daniel. *The Reforming of General Education: The Columbia College Experience in Its National Setting.* New York: Columbia University Press, 1966.

Bender, Thomas, ed. *The University and the City: From Medieval Origins to the Present*. New York: Oxford University Press, 1988.

Benedict, Ruth. *Patterns of Culture*. Boston: Houghton Mifflin, 1934.

Bidney, David. "The Concept of Value in Modern Anthropology." In *Anthropology Today: An Encyclopedic Inventory*, International Symposium on Anthropology, with a preface by Paul Fejos and intro. A. L. Kroeber, pp. 682–99. Chicago: University of Chicago Press, 1953.

———. *Theoretical Anthropology*. 2nd, augmented ed. New York: Schocken, 1967 [1953].

Bishop, Morris. *A History of Cornell*. Ithaca, N.Y.: Cornell University Press, 1966.

Bloom, Allan. *The Closing of the American Mind: How Higher Education Has Failed Democracy and Impoverished the Souls of Today's Students*. New York: Simon and Schuster, 1987.

Boas, Franz. *The Mind of Primitive Man*, rev. ed. New York: Macmillan, 1938 [1911].

Bromwich, David. *Politics by Other Means: Higher Education and Group Thinking*. New Haven, Conn.: Yale University Press, 1992.

Buchler, Justus. "Reconstruction in the Liberal Arts." In Dwight C. Miner, ed., *A History of Columbia College on Morningside*, pp. 48–135. New York: Columbia University Press, 1954.

Buck, Paul H. "Report of the Faculty of Arts and Sciences." *Official Register of Harvard University* 45 (May 20, 1948): 32–46.

Cathcart, Arthur Martin. "Constitutional Freedom of Speech and of the Press." Typescript, Stanford University Libraries, 323.443/C362. Delivered to the Commonwealth Club, Mar. 29, 1935.

———. "What Is Happening to the Constitution?" Typescript, Stanford University Libraries, 342.73/C362. Delivered to the Commonwealth Club, Oct. 20, 1933.

Channing, William Ellery. *The Perfect Life: In Twelve Discourses*, ed. William Henry Channing. Boston: Roberts, 1873.

Clark, J. B. "Preparation for Citizenship at Smith College." *Education* 9 (Feb. 1889): 403–6.

Cockburn, Henry Cockburn, Lord. *Memorials of His Time*, ed. W. Forbes Gray. Edinburgh: Robert Graf & Son, 1946 [1856].

Copleston, Edward. *Advice to a Young Reviewer, with a Specimen of the Art*. In George Gordon, ed., *Three Oxford Ironies*, pp. 49–75. London: Humphrey Milford, 1927.

———. *A Reply to the Calumnies of the "Edinburgh Review" Against Oxford*. Oxford: Printed for the Author, 1810.

Court, Franklin E. *Institutionalizing English Literature: The Culture and Politics of Literary Study, 1750–1900.* Stanford, Calif.: Stanford University Press, 1992.

Cowley, Malcolm. "Humanizing Society." In C. Hartley Grattan, ed., *The Critique of Humanism: A Symposium,* pp. 63–84. New York: Brewer and Warren, 1930.

Crehore, C. F., M.D. "The Teaching of Civics in Schools." *Education* 7 (Dec. 1886): 264–65.

Darcy, Anthony. "Franz Boas and the Concept of Culture: A Genealogy." In Diane J. Austin-Broos, ed., *Creating Culture: Profiles in the Study of Culture,* pp. 3–17. Sydney: Allen & Unwin, 1987.

Debs, Eugene V. "The Cry of 'Anarchist.'" *American Magazine of Civics* 6 (Jan.–June 1895): 408–12.

DeLaura, David J. "Matthew Arnold and Culture: The History and the Prehistory." In Clinton Machann and Forrest D. Burt, eds., *Matthew Arnold in His Time and Ours: Centenary Essays,* pp. 1–16. Charlottesville: University Press of Virginia, 1988.

Dewey, John. "American Education and Culture." In John Dewey, *Characters and Events: Popular Essays in Social and Political Philosophy,* ed. Joseph Ratner, 2: 498–503. New York: Henry Holt, 1929.

D'Souza, Dinesh. *Illiberal Education.* New York: Free Press, 1991.

Edgeworth, Richard Lovell. *Essays on Professional Education,* 2nd ed. London: Johnson, 1812 [1809].

Eliot, Charles William. "Liberty in Education." In Charles William Eliot, *Educational Reform: Essays and Addresses,* pp. 123–48. New York: Century, 1898.

———. "What Is a Liberal Education?" In Charles William Eliot, *Educational Reform: Essays and Addresses,* pp. 87–122. New York: Century, 1898.

———, ed. *The Harvard Classics.* New York: P. F. Collier, 1910.

Engel, Arthur. "Emerging Concepts of the Academic Profession at Oxford 1800–1854." In Lawrence Stone, ed., *The University in Society* 1: 305–51. Princeton, N.J.: Princeton University Press, 1974.

Erskine, John. *The Delight of Great Books.* Indianapolis: Bobbs-Merrill, 1928.

———. *The Influence of Women and Its Cure.* Indianapolis: Bobbs-Merrill, 1936.

———. "Magic and Wonder in Literature." In John Erskine, *"The Moral Obligation to Be Intelligent" and Other Essays,* pp. 119–67. New York: Duffield, 1916.

Farrand, Max. "Report of the Conference on History in the College

Curriculum." *Annual Report of the American Historical Association for the Year 1906* 1: 105–25.

Farrar, F. W. *Great Books: Bunyan, Shakespeare, Dante, Milton, The Imitation, Etc.* London: Isbister, 1898.

———, ed. *Essays on a Liberal Education.* 2nd ed. London: Macmillan, 1868 [1867].

Foerster, Norman, ed. *Humanism and America: Essays on the Outlook of Modern Civilisation.* New York: Farrar and Rinehart, 1930.

Forman, S. E. *Advanced Civics: The Spirit, the Form, and the Functions of the American Government.* New York: Century, 1910 [1905].

Garland, Martha McMackin. *Cambridge Before Darwin: The Ideal of a Liberal Education, 1800–1860.* Cambridge, Eng.: Cambridge University Press, 1980.

Geertz, Clifford. "Blurred Genres: The Refiguration of Social Thought." *American Scholar* 49 (Spring 1980): 165–79.

General Education in a Free Society: Report of the Harvard Committee, intro. James Bryant Conant. Cambridge, Mass.: Harvard University Press, 1945.

Gibson, William. *Neuromancer.* New York: Ace Science Fiction Books, 1984.

Gideonse, Harry D. *The Higher Learning in a Democracy: A Reply to President Hutchins' Critique of the American University.* New York: Farrar and Rinehart, 1937.

Goodale, Wilmot H. "Patriotism." *American Magazine of Civics* 6 (Jan.–June 1895): 355–68.

Gossett, Thomas F. *Race: The History of an Idea in America.* Dallas: Southern Methodist University Press, 1963.

Graff, Gerald. *Professing Literature: An Institutional History.* Chicago: University of Chicago Press, 1987.

Graff, Gerald, and Michael Warner, eds. *The Origins of Literary Studies in America: A Documentary Anthology.* New York: Routledge, 1989.

Grindal, T. Bruce, and Dennis M. Warren, eds. *Essays in Humanistic Anthropology: A Festschrift in Honor of David Bidney.* Washington, D.C.: University Press of America, 1979.

Guitteau, William Backus. *Preparing for Citizenship: An Elementary Textbook in Civics.* Boston: Houghton Mifflin, 1913.

Hamilton, Sir William. *Discussions on Philosophy and Literature, Education and University Reform.* 3rd ed. Edinburgh and London: William Blackwood, 1866 [1852].

Hart, Albert Bushnell. "Preparation for Citizenship at Harvard College." *Education* 8 (June 1888): 630–38.

Hart, James Morgan. "The College Course in English Literature, How It May Be Improved." *Transactions of the Modern Language Association* 1 (1884–85): 84–95.

Harvard: 1956. Special issue of *i.e.: The Cambridge Review* (June 1956).

Haskins, Charles H. "Report of the Conference on the First Year of College Work in History." *Annual Report of the American Historical Association for the Year 1905* 1: 147–74.

Hawkins, Hugh. *Between Harvard and America: The Educational Leadership of Charles W. Eliot.* New York: Oxford University Press, 1972.

Herbert, Christopher. *Culture and Anomie: Ethnographic Imagination in the Nineteenth Century.* Chicago: University of Chicago Press, 1991.

Higham, John. *Strangers in the Land: Patterns of American Nativism 1860–1925.* New York: Atheneum, 1963 [1955].

Hirsch, E. D. *Cultural Literacy: What Every American Needs to Know.* Boston: Houghton Mifflin, 1987.

Hofstadter, Richard, and Wilson Smith, eds. *American Higher Education: A Documentary History.* Chicago: University of Chicago Press, 1961.

Howe, M. A. DeWolfe. *Barrett Wendell and His Letters.* Boston: Atlantic Monthly, 1924.

Hunt, Theodore W. "The Place of English in the College Curriculum." *Transactions of the Modern Language Association* 1 (1884–85): 118–32.

Hutchins, Robert Maynard. *The Great Conversation: The Substance of a Liberal Education.* Vol. 1 of Robert Maynard Hutchins, ed., *Great Books of the Western World.* Chicago: Encyclopedia Britannica, 1952.

———. *The Higher Learning in America.* New Haven, Conn.: Yale University Press, 1936.

Huxley, Thomas H. "A Liberal Education; and Where to Find It." In Thomas H. Huxley, *Science and Education,* pp. 76–110. New York: D. Appleton, 1896 [1893].

"Initiatory Courses for Freshmen." Report by Committee G. *Bulletin of the American Association of University Professors* 8 (Oct. 1922): 10–40.

James, Henry. *Charles W. Eliot: President of Harvard University 1869–1909.* Boston: Houghton Mifflin, 1930.

Johnson, Lesley. *The Cultural Critics: From Matthew Arnold to Raymond Williams.* London: Routledge & Kegan Paul, 1979.

Jordan, David Starr. *The Days of a Man: Being Memories of a Naturalist,*

Teacher and Minor Prophet of Democracy. Yonkers-on-Hudson, N.Y.: World, 1922.

Keller, Phyllis. *Getting at the Core: Curricular Reform at Harvard.* Cambridge, Mass.: Harvard University Press, 1982.

Ker, Ian. *John Henry Newman: A Biography.* Oxford: Clarendon Press, 1988.

Kimball, Bruce A. *Orators and Philosophers: A History of the Idea of Liberal Education.* New York: Teachers College Press, Columbia University, 1986.

Kimball, Roger. *Tenured Radicals: How Politics Has Corrupted Our Higher Education.* New York: Harper, 1990.

[Knight, Richard Payne.] Review of Thomas Falconer, ed., *Strabonis Rerum Geographicarum Libri XVII. Edinburgh Review* 28 (July 1809): 429–41.

[Knight, Richard Payne, John Playfair, and Sydney Smith.] Review of Edward Copleston, *A Reply to the Calumnies of the "Edinburgh Review" Against Oxford. Edinburgh Review* 29 (April 1810): 158–87.

Light, Richard J. *The Harvard Assessment Seminars: Second Report,* 1992.

Lindenberger, Herbert. "On the Sacrality of Reading Lists: The Western Culture Debate at Stanford University." In Herbert Lindenberger, *The History of Literature: On Value, Genre, Institutions,* pp. 148–62. New York: Columbia University Press, 1990.

Lougee, Carolyn. "Comment" on Allardyce, "The Rise and Fall of the Western Civilization Course." *American Historical Review* 87 (June 1982): 726–29.

Lyell, Charles. *Travels in North America; with Geological Observations on the United States, Canada, and Nova Scotia.* London: John Murray, 1845.

McBride, Mary G. "Matthew Arnold and Andrew Carnegie: The Religion of Culture and the Gospel of Wealth." In Clinton Machann and Forrest D. Burt, eds., *Matthew Arnold in His Time and Ours: Centenary Essays,* pp. 57–70. Charlottesville: University Press of Virginia, 1988.

McCosh, James. *The New Departure in College Education, Being a Reply to President Eliot's Defense of It in New York, Feb. 24, 1885.* New York: Charles Scribner's Sons, 1885.

MacKibbin, Stuart. "Preparation for Citizenship in Michigan." *Education* 10 (Mar. 1890): 405–13.

McNeill, William H. *Hutchins' University: A Memoir of the University of Chicago 1929–1950.* Chicago: University of Chicago Press, 1991.

Menand, Louis. "What Are Universities For?" *Harper's* 283 (Dec. 1991): 47–56.

Miner, Dwight C., ed. *A History of Columbia College on Morningside.* New York: Columbia University Press, 1954.

Morgan, Lewis Henry. *Ancient Society or Researches in the Lines of Human Progress from Savagery Through Barbarism to Civilization,* ed. Leslie A. White. Cambridge, Mass.: Harvard University Press, 1964 [1877].

Morison, Samuel Eliot. *Three Centuries of Harvard, 1636–1936.* Cambridge, Mass.: Harvard University Press, 1942.

Morse, Anson D. "Preparation for Citizenship at Amherst College." *Education* 9 (Dec. 1888): 236–46.

Munro, Dana Carleton, and George Clarke Sellery, trans. and eds. *Mediaeval Civilization: Selected Studies from European Authors.* New York: Century, 1904.

"A National Reform League." *New York Times,* May 9, 1876, p. 2.

"New CIV Courses in the Works." *The Stanford Daily,* Mar. 3, 1992, p. 1.

Newman, John Henry. *The Idea of a University Defined and Illustrated,* ed. I. T. Ker. Oxford: Clarendon Press, 1976.

Novick, Peter. *That Noble Dream: The "Objectivity Question" and the American Historical Profession.* Cambridge, Eng.: Cambridge University Press, 1988.

Paine, Robert Treat. "The Problems of Charity." *American Magazine of Civics* 8 (Jan.–June 1896): 311–20.

Pelikan, Jaroslav. *The Idea of the University: A Reexamination.* New Haven, Conn.: Yale University Press, 1992.

Perry, Arthur Latham. "Preparation for Citizenship at Williams College." *Education* 9 (Apr. 1889): 513–21.

[Playfair, John.] Review of P. S. Laplace, *Traité de Méchanique Céleste. Edinburgh Review* 22 (Jan. 1808): 249–84.

Puddefoot, W. G. "Is the Foreigner a Menace to the Nation?" *American Magazine of Civics* 9 (Jul. 1896–Jan. 1897): 1–11.

Raleigh, John Henry. *Matthew Arnold and American Culture.* University of California English Studies 17. Berkeley: University of California Press, 1957.

Rand, E. K. "Harvard's New Liberal Arts." Typescript, Harvard University Archives, HUC 8945.74.

Randall, John Herman. *The Making of the Modern Mind: A Survey of the Intellectual Background of the Present Age.* Boston: Houghton Mifflin, 1926.

Redfield, Robert. *The Primitive World and Its Transformations*. Ithaca, N.Y.: Cornell University Press, 1953.

Reuben, Julie A. "In Search of Truth: Scientific Inquiry, Religion, and the Development of the American University, 1870–1920." Ph.D. diss., Stanford University, 1990.

Rothblatt, Sheldon. *The Idea of the Idea of a University and Its Antithesis*. Bundoora, Victoria, Australia: Seminar on the Sociology of Culture, La Trobe University, 1989.

———. "A Long Apocrypha of Inquiry: The Humanities and Humanity." *Mosaic* 23 (1990): 1–14.

———. "Modern Citizenship and Mass Higher Educational Systems in the United States." In Brita Rang and Jan C. C. Rupp, eds. *The Cultural Range of Citizenship: Citizenship and Education in England, Scotland, Germany, the United States and the Netherlands*, pp. 33–44. Utrecht: ISOR, 1991.

———. "The Student Sub-culture and the Examination System in Early 19th Century Oxbridge." In Lawrence Stone, ed., *The University in Society*, 1: 247–303. Princeton, N.J.: Princeton University Press, 1974.

———. *Tradition and Change in English Liberal Education: An Essay in History and Culture*. London: Faber and Faber, 1976.

Rudolph, Frederick. *The American College and University: A History*. New York: Random House, 1962.

———. *Curriculum: A History of the American Undergraduate Course of Study Since 1636*. San Francisco: Jossey-Bass, 1977.

Sapir, Edward. "Culture, Genuine and Spurious." In *Selected Writings of Edward Sapir in Language, Culture and Personality*, ed. David G. Mandelbaum, pp. 308–31. Berkeley: University of California Press, 1963.

Searle, John. "The Storm over the University." *New York Review of Books* 37 (Dec. 6, 1990): 34–42.

Sidgwick, Henry. "The Theory of Classical Education." In F. W. Farrar, ed., *Essays on a Liberal Education*, pp. 81–143. London: Macmillan, 1868.

Slee, Peter R. H. *Learning and a Liberal Education: The Study of Modern History in the Universities of Oxford, Cambridge, and Manchester, 1800–1914*. Manchester: Manchester University Press, 1986.

———. "The Oxford Idea of a Liberal Education 1800–1860: The Invention of Tradition and the Manufacture of Practice." *History of Universities* 7 (1988): 61–87.

Smith, Adam. *An Inquiry into the Nature and Causes of the Wealth of*

Nations. London: W. Strahan and T. Cadell, 1776.

[Smith, Sydney.] Review of Richard Lovell Edgeworth, *Essays on Professional Education*. *Edinburgh Review* 29 (Oct. 1809): 40–53.

Solomon, Barbara. *Ancestors and Immigrants: A Changing New England Tradition*. Cambridge, Mass.: Harvard University Press, 1956.

Stocking, George W., Jr. "Matthew Arnold, E. B. Tylor, and the Uses of Invention." In *Race, Culture, and Evolution: Essays in the History of Anthropology*, pp. 69–90. New York: Free Press, 1968.

The Study of Education at Stanford: Report to the University. Nov. 1968.

Suksdorf, Henry F. *Our Race Problems*. New York: Shakespeare Press, 1911.

Sumner, William Graham. Letter "to the Members of the Corporation and to the permanent officers of Yale College," June 1881. In Richard Hofstadter and Wilson Smith, eds., *American Higher Education: A Documentary History* 2: 850–57. Chicago: University of Chicago Press, 1961.

Sutton, Preston M. "Speech in Behalf of the Bill Relating to a Course of Study for the State Agricultural College." In Richard Hofstadter and Wilson Smith, eds., *American Higher Education: A Documentary History* 2: 587–92. Chicago: University of Chicago Press, 1961.

Tate, Allen. "The Fallacy of Humanism." In C. Hartley Grattan, ed., *The Critique of Humanism: A Symposium*, pp. 131–66. New York: Brewer and Warren, 1930.

The Idea and Practice of General Education: An Account of the College of the University of Chicago By Present and Former Members of the Faculty, ed. F. Champion Ward. With a new Preface by Donald N. Levine. Chicago: University of Chicago Press, 1992 [1950].

Thomas, Vaughan. *The Legality of the Present Academical System of the University of Oxford Asserted Against the New Calumnies of the "Edinburgh Review"*. Oxford: J. Parker, 1831.

Tyack, David B. *George Ticknor and the Boston Brahmins*. Cambridge, Mass: Harvard University Press, 1967.

Tylor, Edward B. *Primitive Culture: Researches into the Development of Mythology, Philosophy, Religion, Language, Art and Custom*, 3rd American, from the 2nd English Edition. New York: Henry Holt, 1889 [1871].

Veblen, Thorstein. *The Higher Learning in America: A Memorandum on the Conduct of Universities by Business Men*. New York: B. W. Huebsch, 1918.

Veysey, Laurence R. *The Emergence of the American University*. Chicago: University of Chicago Press, 1965.

"Waite, Henry Randall." *Appleton's Cyclopaedia of American Biography* 6: 318.

Waite, Henry Randall. "Civics: A Science for Citizens and a Creed for Patriots." *American Magazine of Civics* 6 (Jan.–June 1895): 202–5.

———, ed. "The Civic Outlook." *American Magazine of Civics* 8 (Jan.– June 1896): 211–24, 321–36.

Ward, W. R. *Victorian Oxford.* London: Frank Cass, 1965.

Weber, Max. *Max Weber on Universities: The Power of the State and the Dignity of the Academic Calling in Imperial Germany,* trans. and ed. Edward Shils. Chicago: University of Chicago Press, 1974.

Wegener, Charles. *Liberal Education and the Modern University.* Chicago: University of Chicago Press, 1978.

Wendell, Barrett. "De Praeside Magnifico." *Harvard Graduates' Magazine* 18 (Sept. 1909): 15–18.

Wertenbaker, Thomas. *Princeton 1746–1896.* Princeton, N.J.: Princeton University Press, 1946.

Whewell, William. *Of a Liberal Education in General; and with Particular Reference to the Leading Studies of the University of Cambridge.* London: John W. Parker, 1845.

———. *On the Principles of English University Education.* London: John W. Parker, 1837.

———. *Thoughts on the Study of Mathematics, as a Part of a Liberal Education.* Cambridge, Eng.: J & J. J. Deighton, 1835.

Wiener, Norbert. *Cybernetics; or Control and Communication in the Animal and the Machine,* 2nd ed. New York: M.I.T. Press and John Wiley, 1961 [1948].

———. *The Human Use of Human Beings: Cybernetics and Society.* Boston: Houghton Mifflin, 1950.

Williams, Raymond. *Culture and Society 1780–1950.* New York: Columbia University Press, 1958.

Wilson, Edmund. "Notes on Babbitt and More." In C. Hartley Grattan, ed., *The Critique of Humanism: A Symposium,* pp. 39–60. New York: Brewer and Warren, 1930.

Wilson, Woodrow. "Mere Literature." In Woodrow Wilson, *"Mere Literature" and Other Essays,* pp. 1–27. Boston: Houghton Mifflin, 1896.

———. "The Spirit of Learning." *Harvard Graduates' Magazine* 18 (Sept. 1909): 1–14.

Winters, Yvor. "Poetry, Morality, and Criticism." In C. Hartley Grattan, ed., *The Critique of Humanism: A Symposium,* pp. 301–33. New York: Brewer and Warren, 1930.

Woodberry, George Edward. *Great Writers*. New York: Macmillan, 1912 [1907].

———. *The Torch: Eight Lectures on Race Power in Literature Delivered Before the Lowell Institute of Boston MCMIII*. New York: Macmillan, 1912 [1905].

Index

In this index an "f" after a number indicates a separate reference on the next page, and an "ff" indicates separate references on the next two pages. A continuous discussion over two or more pages is indicated by a span of page numbers, e.g., "pp. 57–58." *Passim* is used for a cluster of references in close but not consecutive sequence.

Adams, Charles Francis, 56–59, 63, 88
Adler, Mortimer, 85, 90
Agassiz, Louis, 13
Allardyce, Gilbert, 61, 98–99
American Democracy in Time of Crisis (Robinson), 130–31, 144
American Historical Association, 60–61, 69, 98
American Magazine of Civics, 73–74
Amherst College, 72
Ancient Society (Morgan), 104
Andrews, E. Benjamin, 74
Anthropology, 103–10, 119–20
Aquinas, Thomas, 93
Aristotle, 24f, 93
Arnold, Matthew, 3, 21, 42–43, 80, 84, 98, 152n24; on liberal education, 24, 38; humanism of, 38, 40, 63f, 66; *Culture and Anarchy* by, 39–40, 46–49; on Oxford education, 39–40, 46; on American culture, 46–49, 56; and cultural anthropology, 103–6, 110
Arnold, Thomas, 132
Assessment seminars, 154n10
Augustine, Saint, 102, 119, 125

Babbitt, Irving, 24, 63–67, 80, 88, 108, 124
Bacon, Francis, 22, 24, 63
Becker, Carl, 13
Beer, Samuel, 116
Bell, Daniel, 4, 92
Benedict, Ruth, 108–9
Bentham, Jeremy, 93
Bentley, Richard, 23
Berkeley, William, 143
Bible, 93, 119
Bidney, David, 107–8

Bishop, Morris, 48
Blackmur, R. P., 65
Bloom, Allan, 3, 40–41, 86
Boas, Franz, 103, 105–6, 108ff, 130
Bodin, Jean, 93
Bok, Derek, 154n10
Bradford, William, 49
Bright, John, 47
Bromwich, David, 149n5
Bryce, James, 130
Buck, Paul, 92
Bureaucracy, 6, 41
Burke, Edmund, 16, 23
Burke, Kenneth, 65
Bush, George, 1–2

Calvinism, 54, 150n6
Cambridge University: liberal education at, 1, 21, 35–36, 53; McCosh's praise of, 20–21; scientific learning at, 34ff; classical literature at, 35, 37, 55, 80, 117
Canon, literary, 119f, 125. *See also* "Great books" curriculum
Carnegie, Andrew, 49
Cathcart, Arthur Martin, 77, 119
Catholicism, 41–42, 43f, 50
Catholic University, in Ireland, 40–41
Cervantes, Miguel de, 81
Channing, William Ellery, 54–55, 150n6
Channing, William Henry, 150n6
Chaucer, Geoffrey, 82
Citizenship, courses in, 69–79, 87, 151n11; at Stanford University, 70ff, 77–78, 87, 103, 113, 120, 129–44
Civics, 72–75, 114, 117–18, 151n11
Claremont Colleges, 57

Classical literature, 62, 64f, 76, 93, 148n10, 150n7; at Oxford University, 26–27, 29–30, 55, 64, 80; at Cambridge University, 35, 37, 55, 80
The Closing of the American Mind (Bloom), 3, 40–41
Clough, Arthur Hugh, 47
Colonialism, 105
Columbia University, 4, 56f, 85, 92, 94, 106, 114, 135; "Contemporary Civilization" course at, 55f, 68, 70, 76–78, 87, 90, 93, 107, 115
Commercialism, 29f, 117
Commonwealth Club of California, 77
Communism, 108, 140
Conant, James Bryant, 90
Copernican system, 101, 103f, 110
Copleston, Edward, 27–30, 32, 39, 65
Core curriculum, 116, 122
Cornell, Ezra, 12, 47–48, 120
Cornell University, 2, 7, 12f, 47–48, 51–52
Cowley, Malcolm, 65
Crisis mentality, 3–4, 6f
Croly, Herbert, 136
Cultural anthropology, 103–10, 119–20
Cultural Literacy (Hirsch), 122
Culture and Anarchy (Arnold), 39–40, 46–49

Dante Alighieri, 67, 80, 93, 117ff
Dartmouth College, 70ff, 135
Darwin, Charles, 13, 58f, 63f, 119
Darwinism, 1, 13–14, 15–16, 20, 63, 104
Debs, Eugene V., 74

Democracy, 1, 3, 24, 51, 89–90, 108, 121, 138, 142–43
Dewey, John, 23, 88, 107, 130
Dick, Philip K., 125
Distribution requirements, 18–19, 20, 96, 116–17
D'Souza, Dinesh, 102
Duruy, Victor, 9

Edgeworth, Richard Lovell, 25f, 29, 148n10
Edinburgh Review, 25–34 *passim*, 117, 149n22
Edwards, Jonathan, 54, 150n6
Egalitarianism, 1, 4
Eliot, Charles William, 48ff, 88, 94f, 123, 125, 144; and English educational model, 2–3, 24; and free elective system, 2f, 5, 9–18, 20f, 51, 53, 55, 58, 72, 120; and German educational model, 2, 5; as Harvard president, 2–3, 9–10, 12, 15, 36, 51–55, 57f, 63, 91f, 97, 121; and Unitarianism, 5, 15f, 49; and debate with James McCosh, 10–22 *passim*, 40, 48, 62; and social Darwinism, 13–22 *passim*; and relations with Barrett Wendell, 52–55, 63, 150n6; and neo-humanism, 63–67; on literary classics, 67, 80f, 86
Eliot, T. S., 65
Ellison, Ralph, 118
Emerson, Ralph Waldo, 13, 79f, 119
Encyclopaedia Britannica, 86
Engineering, 36, 124, 135
Enlightenment, 13, 24, 42, 103
Erskine, John, 79–88 *passim*, 106
Essays on a Liberal Education

(Farrar), 55, 80
Ethnocentrism, 104–5, 109

Falconer, Thomas, 25–26
Farrand, Max, 61
Farrar, F. W., 55, 80–81
Fascism, 107f, 140
Fiction, 67, 115, 125
Flexner, Abraham, 17
Foerster, Norman, 65
Forman, Samuel Eagle, 75
Franklin, Benjamin, 119
Free elective system: Eliot's advocacy of, 2f, 5, 9–18, 20f, 51, 53, 55, 58, 72, 120; instituted at Harvard, 2f, 5, 9–18, 20f, 72; and liberal education, 3, 5, 10–11, 53; and Eliot-McCosh debate, 10–11, 12, 16–21, 48; and self-government, 11–12, 13, 18; "mechanical" constraints on, 12–13; and social Darwinism, 13–18 *passim*; and distribution requirements, 18–19, 20, 116; and *laissez-faire*, 19–20; repudiated at Harvard, 51–58 *passim*, 64, 67
Freeman, Edward Augustus, 104
Freud, Sigmund, 119, 125
Fuller, Margaret, 47

Galileo Galilei, 125
Garfield, James A., 134–35
Geertz, Clifford, 110
General Education in a Free Society, see Redbook study
Gentlemanly virtues, 43–44
German universities, 2, 5
Gibbon, Edward, 9, 26, 69
Gibson, William, 125
Gideonse, Harry D., 88–90, 94

Gilman, Daniel Coit, 7, 52
Gobineau, Joseph-Arthur de, 82
Goodale, Wilmot H., 73–74
Gossett, Thomas F., 82, 151–52n24
Grattan, C. Hartley, 65
"Great books" curriculum, 79–
 87, 92–93, 99, 106, 109, 118,
 120, 152n24; elaborated by
 Hutchins, 80, 85–86, 90, 152n32
Guitteau, William Backus, 74–75

Hadley, Arthur Twining, 143
Hamilton, William, 30–34, 65,
 85, 90
Harper, William Rainey, 7
Hart, Albert Bushnell, 72, 151n7
The Harvard Classics, 67
Harvard: 1956, 95–97
Harvard University, 7, 19; Eliot
 as president of, 2–3, 9–10, 12,
 15, 36, 51–55, 57f, 63, 91f, 97, 121;
 free election instituted at, 2f, 5,
 9–18, 20f, 72; liberal education
 at, 3, 5, 10–11, 53; Lyell and, 34–
 35; free election repudiated at,
 51–58 *passim*, 64, 67; Adams's
 reorganization scheme for, 56–
 59; history courses at, 69f, 72;
 Redbook study of, 89, 90–96,
 107f, 116, 122; students' critique
 of curriculum at, 95–97; distribution requirements at, 96,
 116; cultural anthropology at,
 108–9; core curriculum at, 116,
 122, 124; compared to Stanford
 University, 123–24; assessment
 seminars at, 154n10
Haskins, Charles Homer, 59, 61,
 70, 88, 98
Hegel, G. W. F., 23
Higham, John, 69

*The Higher Learning in a Democ-
 racy* (Gideonse), 88–90
The Higher Learning in America
 (Hutchins), 85, 88
The Higher Learning in America
 (Veblen), 88, 114
Hirsch, E. D., 122f
History, as academic discipline,
 35, 55–56, 58–61, 66, 103; and
 Western civilization courses,
 61, 69–71, 76, 98
Hobbes, Thomas, 125
Hofstadter, Richard, 4
Homer, 67, 81, 93, 119
Hoover, Herbert, 130
Horace, 23
Humanism, 38, 40, 42, 47, 50;
 and neo-humanism, 63–67,
 79f, 87
Humanities, 19, 56, 58, 62–67, 85f,
 91f, 101, 115, 150n17
Hunt, Theodore W., 62
Hutchins, Robert Maynard, 17,
 88–90, 94, 99, 121, 123, 152n32;
 and "great books" curriculum,
 80, 85–86, 90, 152n32
Huxley, Thomas Henry, 115

The Idea of a University (Newman), 39–46
i.e.: The Cambridge Review, 95
Illiberal Education (D'Souza),
 102
Immigration, 1, 17, 69, 72, 83,
 114, 151n7

James, William, 107
Jefferson, Thomas, 23
Jeffrey, Francis, 30
Johns Hopkins University, 7,
 52, 135

Johnson, Barbara, 42–43, 149n5
Jordan, David Starr, 13, 15, 51–52, 130, 141
Joyce, James, 115

Kant, Immanuel, 33, 107
Keynes, John Maynard, 130
Kimball, Roger, 42–43, 46
Knight, Richard Payne, 25

Languages, academic study of, 18, 20, 55, 61–65
Laplace, Pierre-Simon, 25
Laski, Harold, 130
Leavis, F. R., 109
Legal profession, 36, 135
Lindenberger, Herbert, 10
Lippmann, Walter, 130
Literature, academic study of, 18, 20f, 44–45, 58–67, 103; classical, 26–27, 29–30, 35, 37, 55, 62, 64f, 71, 93; modern, 35, 55–56, 62, 64, 66; and neo-humanism, 63–67, 79f, 87; and "great books" curriculum, 79–87, 92–93; and New Criticism, 81, 115
Locke, John, 22, 24, 93, 107
Lowell, A. Lawrence, 53, 114
Lucretius, 79
Luther, Martin, 93, 119
Lyell, Charles, 34–38
Lynd, Robert S., 130

McCosh, James, 88, 101; and debate with Charles Eliot, 10–11, 12, 16–21, 22, 40, 48, 59, 62; as Princeton president, 16, 52; on pedagogical "trinitarianism," 18–19, 40, 48
Machiavelli, Niccolò, 93

McNeill, William, 121
The Making of the Modern Mind (Randall), 77
Malory, Thomas, 82
Marxism, 109
Mass culture, 109
Mathematics, 20, 25, 35, 37, 55, 58f, 117
Maurice, F. D., 152n24
Medical profession, 29, 36, 135
Medieval history, 69, 71, 119
Meiklejohn, Alexander, 136
Menand, Louis, 7
Military education, 29
Mill, John Stuart, 80, 93
Mills College, 123
Milton, John, 27, 80ff, 84f, 93, 104
The Mind of Primitive Man (Boas), 106, 130
Misogyny, 84–85
Modern Language Association, 61–62
Montaigne, Michel de, 81
Montesquieu, Baron de La Brède et de, 93
Moral philosophy, 32, 42–43, 58–59
More, Paul Elmer, 65f
Morgan, Lewis Henry, 104f
Morison, Samuel Eliot, 17, 95
Multiculturalism, 3, 118, 125
Mumford, Lewis, 65
Munro, Dana C., 71, 76, 119
Munro, William Bennett, 131

Napier, Macvey, 30, 149n22
Nativism, 16, 82, 114
Natural sciences, 23–24, 91ff, 125; and tripartite academic structure, 18–19, 58, 62, 92, 150n17; at Oxford University, 25, 35–36;

at Cambridge University, 34ff;
and liberal education, 34–37
Nazism, 107f
Neilson, William Allan, 67
Neo-humanism, 63–67, 79f, 87
New Criticism, 81, 115
Newman, John Henry, 3, 21,
117; on secularism, 12, 40–42,
44–45; on liberal education,
24, 38, 40–46; humanism
of, 38, 40, 50; *Idea of a University* by, 39–46, 148n24; as
Catholic University president,
40–41; on virtue, 42–44; on
sinfulness, 44, 49, 117
Newton, Isaac, 19, 58
Niebuhr, Reinhold, 90

Oxford University: liberal education at, 1, 21, 25–33, 36, 53;
as model for American educational reform, 2, 57; McCosh's
praise of, 20–21; "modernist"
critique of, 25–33, 117; scientific
learning at, 25, 35–36; classical
literature at, 26–27, 29–30, 55,
64, 80, 117; Copleston's defense of, 27–30, 32, 39; Arnold's
praise of, 39–40, 46; Newman
at, 39–40

Packer, Herbert L., 97
Paine, Robert Treat, 74
Paine, Thomas, 23
Paradise Lost (Milton), 104
Patriotism, 73–74
Patterns of Culture (Benedict),
108–9
Peel, Robert, 41
Pelikan, Jaroslav, 7
Philanthropy, 74
Philology, 33, 62, 64, 66

Philosophy, 18, 20f, 31–34, 55,
62, 70
Plato, 22, 66, 93, 119
Playfair, John, 25
Poincaré, Henri, 130
Pope, Alexander, 23
Porter, Noah, 20
Presbyterianism, 16, 18
Prescriptive system, 16, 18–21;
and distribution requirements,
18–19, 20, 96, 116–17; and Red-
book study, 90–96, 116, 122;
and core curriculum, 116, 122
Primitive Culture (Tylor), 103–5
Princeton University, 10, 20f,
54; McCosh as president of,
16, 40; tripartite academic
structure at, 18–19, 40
Professional disciplines, 29–30,
36, 117, 135
Ptolemaic system, 19, 101, 104, 110
Puddefoot, W. G., 73
Puritanism, 20, 48, 67

Race relations, 16, 82–84, 106,
139, 151–52n24
Rand, E. K., 94
Randall, John Herman, 77, 130
Redbook study, 89, 90–96, 107f,
116, 122
Redfield, Robert, 107
*The Reforming of General Educa-
tion* (Bell), 92
Renaissance, 24
Renan, Ernest, 47
Required reading lists, 117,
119, 125
Research university, 4, 6, 37, 51
Rhodes, James Ford, 150n6
Robinson, Edgar Eugene, 77–78,
113, 129–44
Romanticism, 79f, 108

Rosovsky, Henry, 116
Rothblatt, Sheldon, 26, 29, 148n24
Rousseau, Jean-Jacques, 22, 24, 26, 63, 93, 108
Routinization, Weber on, 6
Rudolph, Frederick, 4
Ruhnken, David, 33
Ruskin, John, 81
Russell, Bertrand, 130

Salmon, Lucy M., 69
Sangster, Margaret E., 75
Sapir, Edward, 106
Schlesinger, Arthur M., Sr., 92
Scholasticism, 22
Sciences, *see* Natural sciences; Social sciences
Scotland, educational modernism in, 25, 28, 30, 32
Scott, Walter, 81
Searle, John, 4
Secularism, 12, 16, 18, 40–42, 44–45
Sellery, George C., 71
Sexual freedom, 96–97
Shakespeare, William, 58f, 80, 81–82, 84, 93
Shaler, Nathaniel, 137
Sheeler, Charles, 66
Shelley, Percy Bysshe, 79f, 84
Sidgwick, Henry, 55, 150n7
Smith, Adam, 13–14, 93
Smith, Sydney, 25f
Smith, Wilson, 4
Smith College, 72
Snow, C. P., 125
Social Darwinism, 1, 13–14, 15–16, 17f, 20
Social sciences, 18–19, 58, 70, 91f, 110, 131, 143, 150n17
Solomon, Barbara Miller, 72

Sophocles, 66
Spencer, Herbert, 13–20 *passim*, 59, 63
Spenser, Edmund, 82, 84
Stanford University, 7, 65, 68, 75; "Western Culture" course at, 1, 10, 99, 101–3, 110, 117, 125; Jordan as president of, 13, 51–52; "Problems of Citizenship" course at, 70ff, 77–78, 87, 103, 113, 120, 129–44; "Western Civilization" course at, 71, 76, 78, 98–99, 100–103, 110, 113, 119f, 130; Cathcart committee at, 77, 119; *Study of Education* published at, 89, 97–98, 123; "Culture, Ideas, and Values" course at, 102–3, 110–11, 117; distribution requirements at, 116–17; required reading lists at, 119, 125; compared to Harvard University, 123–24
Sterling, J. E. Wallace, 97
Stewart, Dugald, 9, 28
Stocking, George, 104f
Strabo, 25
Student activism, 95–96
Student government, 11
Study of Education at Stanford, 89, 97–98, 123
Suksdorf, Henry F., 82–83, 106, 152n24
Sumner, William Graham, 20
Sutton, Preston M., 60, 62
Swift, Jonathan, 23, 27, 46
Syracuse University, 135

Tate, Allen, 63, 65
Technology, 23–24, 125
Tenured Radicals (Kimball), 42
Terman, Frederick, 124
Thomas, Vaughn, 30f

Thoreau, Henry David, 119
Ticknor, George, 36, 52
Tolstoy, Leo, 93
Tractarian movement, 35
Trilling, Lionel, 106
Tripartite academic structure,
   18–19, 40, 58, 62, 92, 150n17
Tylor, Edward, 103–6, 109,
   119–20

Unitarianism, 5, 15f, 49
University of California at Santa
   Cruz, 57
University of Chicago, 7, 80,
   85–86, 92, 121, 123, 152n32
University of Minnesota, 69
University of Missouri, 72
University of Wisconsin, 69, 71
Utilitarianism, 23f, 35

Vassar College, 69
Veblen, Thorstein, 88, 114
Veysey, Laurence, 4
Vietnam War, 99
Virgil, 67, 81, 93
Virtues, moral, 42–43

Wagner, Richard, 82
Waite, Henry Randall, 72–73, 74f
Wallas, Graham, 140

Weber, Max, 6, 14
Wegener, Charles, 115, 148n3
Wells, H. G., 141
Wendell, Barrett, 52–55, 82, 150n6,
   152n24
Western civilization, courses in,
   61, 69–71, 76, 78–79, 86–87,
   109, 114–15, 118; at Stanford
   University, 71, 76, 98–99,
   100–103, 113, 119f, 130
Whewell, William, 34, 36–38,
   149n22
White, Andrew Dickson, 2, 13, 51
Wiener, Norbert, 125
Wilbur, Ray Lyman, 77, 144
Williams, Raymond, 109f
Williams College, 72
Wilson, Edmund, 65f
Wilson, James Q., 122, 124
Wilson, Woodrow, 54, 66–67, 73f
Winters, Yvor, 65f
Wollstonecraft, Mary, 125
Woodberry, George Edward, 79,
   81–88 *passim*, 106
Wordsworth, William, 80, 84
World War I, 69–70
World War II, 107f

Yale University, 20, 57, 69

Library of Congress Cataloging-in-Publication Data

Carnochan, W. B.
The battleground of the curriculum : liberal education and
American experience / W. B. Carnochan.
p.   cm.
Includes bibliographical references (p.) and index.
ISBN 0-8047-2147-5 (alk. paper)
1. Education, Higher—United States—Curricula—History.
2. Education, Humanistic—United States—History.
3. Education, Higher—Political aspects—United States—
History. I. Title.
LB2361.5.C38   1993
378.1′99′0973—dc20
92-40401
CIP

∞This book is printed on acid-free paper.
It has been typeset in 10/13 Galliard
by Tseng Information Systems.